Step by Step
Guide to

JEWELRY MAKING

Avril Rodway

HAMLYN
London · New York · Sydney · Toronto

Published by
The Hamlyn Publishing Group Ltd
London · New York · Sydney · Toronto
Astronaut House, Feltham, Middlesex, England

© Copyright The Hamlyn Publishing Group Limited 1973

ISBN 0 600 38071 8

Printed in England by Chapel River Press, Andover, Hampshire

Contents

Introduction

Making costume jewelry is a hobby that snowballs. Once you start, and acquire a few simple techniques, all kinds of ideas will suggest themselves to you, and you'll be surprised at the — on the face of it — unlikely things which end up adorning you and your friends!

This book will give you ideas and instructions for making more than eighty pieces of jewelry, from the more orthodox semi-precious gemstone jewelry — useful to start on as the techniques for applying mounts and findings to stones can be applied to other materials — to such 'fun' makes as jewelry from shells, natural materials and even orange peel.

All the techniques used are very simple, and we have avoided almost entirely asking you to saw, drill or carve any of the materials, except in the most minimal way. Also, the jewelry we suggest is inexpensive in materials and equipment. For instance, we tell you how to make pieces of jewelry using cold set plastic enamels; if you like the results using this comparatively cheap material, you may later want to take up traditional enamelling and buy yourself a small kiln with which to work. Similarly, if gemstones engage your interest, you will perhaps decide to set up a stone tumbler to polish the raw pebbles for yourself.

Much of the material comes from round the house — pasta and pulses from the store cupboard, orange peel, even, strange as it sounds, bones from the stew! Paint, mounts and a little adhesive with, of course, your own skill and taste can transform them all.

1. Gemstone Jewelry

(See colour photograph on p.19)

The popularity of this attractive semi-precious jewelry, which more and more people are making for themselves, has ensured that in most big towns there is a shop or department in a store which sells ready-polished stones and the mounts or 'findings' for turning them into rings, bracelets, pendants, ear-rings of every type. Also needed for this craft are small jewelry pliers, epoxy resin adhesive and, occasionally, a small pair of tweezers. You can find these in the same shop or department.

For a beginner, it is probably best to start by using 'baroque' stones — that is, stones which have an irregular shape, just as they come out of the stone tumbler. They are interesting in appearance, no two being exactly alike in shape, and are cheap to buy, whereas cabochon cut stones — that is stones which are pre-shaped with one flat side and a curved upper surface — or brilliant cut stones with facetted outline are more costly (see diagram 1).

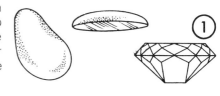

MOUNTS
Look at diagram 2 on p.6 which shows various mounts and findings. This is a general selection of some of the most common ones — you will discover others for yourself. You will see that they are grouped as follows.

Ring mounts
These are nearly always, in the cheaper versions, made so that they can be squeezed together to fit any size of finger. The flat pad type on which can be stuck many kinds of stone are generally very inexpensive and come with a silver, gold or copper finish. Others are available, such as the 'claw' fitting, where points of metal are bent round with pliers to hold the stone firmly in place, or decorative ones for mounting several small stones or providing a cut-out metal edging to the stone.

Bell caps
These come in many different sizes and patterns and are used for making pendants, drop ear-rings or drops for fixing on to bracelets.

Jump rings
Again these are available in a great variety of sizes and shapes. They can be used in many ways — for hanging a pendant on to a neck chain, for fixing together sections of a bracelet, for fixing drop ear-rings on a mount so that they hang in the right way, etc. Spring fastenings are available for fixing necklaces and bracelets.

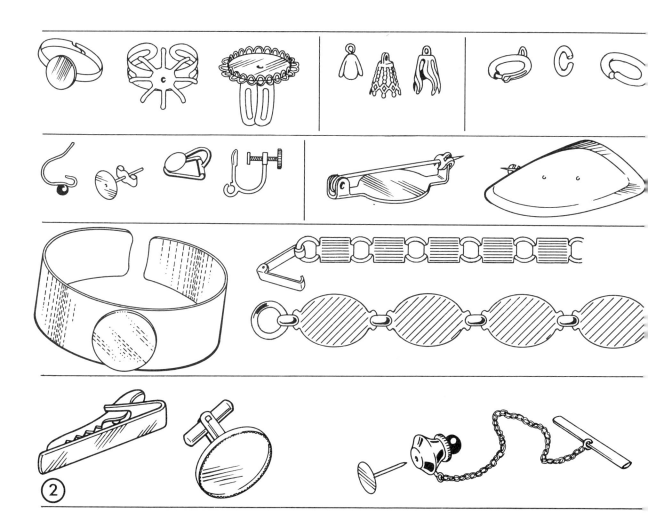

Ear-ring mounts

These vary basically, in that some are for pierced ears and some for unpierced, in which case they have a screw or spring fastening. Some have a tiny ring on which pendant stones can be hung, others a flat pad on which to stick a stone.

Brooch mounts

These can be the round, oval or oblong flat pad type which will be entirely covered by the stone mounted on it, or the decorative kind where an ornamental setting is provided for the stone or stones.

Bracelet mounts

The most usual type of bracelet mount consists of flat pads of different shapes on which the stones are stuck, joined together by links. Some of the pads are small, and the stones cover them completely; others are larger and provide a decorative edging to the stones when they are in place. Chain bracelets for hanging pendant drops are also obtainable, as are wide metal bracelets with a 'display pad' on which a stone can be mounted.

Miscellaneous mounts

Various cuff-link mounts, tie-clips, tie-tacks and key ring mounts can be bought – useful for making presents to give to men.

The subject of mounts is covered in some detail as you will find that they are used for the jewelry described throughout the book. Various copper mounts used in enamel-work can also form a basis for other techniques and will be mentioned in due course.

ADHESIVES

In recent years, the craft of the amateur jewelry maker has been made much simpler by the availability of epoxy resin adhesives. These are generally bought in small packs containing a tube of resin and one of hardener; when mixed together, small quantities at a time and in the proportions recommended by the manufacturer, a chemical reaction takes place causing the adhesive to start hardening, and it finally sets to an extreme hardness and durability (see diagram 3). It will stick glass, metal, wood, china, stones and many other materials, and so is ideal for all kinds of jewelry. Various brands are available, but the one we used for the jewelry shown in this book was Araldite.

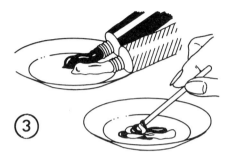

Slight care is needed when working with resin adhesive. For instance, the tube caps must not be mixed or the resin could be 'set off' by a spot of the hardener and the whole tube would set and be unusable. Also it is resistant to all common solvents, so any surplus on your jewelry mount or on the stone you are working with must be removed before it sets. It can be an irritant to sensitive skins, so avoid getting it on your hands as far as possible. If you do, rub it off with detergent powder and rinse in warm water.

When your adhesive is mixed, it can be used for three to five hours before it starts to set hard. Before applying it to your mount or stone, make sure that the surfaces are free from grease – even the small amount which may have come off your fingers from handling them. If they are at all greasy, clean with detergent and dry completely before sticking, then apply a small amount of adhesive with a matchstick to the mount and the stone, and bring both surfaces together. The adhesive should set hard in about twelve hours and develop its full strength after about three days. If the jewelry is left in a warm place, the adhesive will set more quickly.

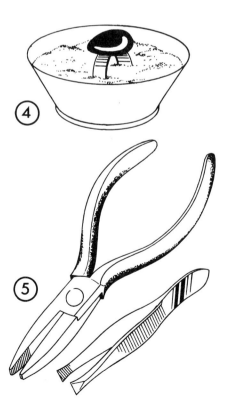

There are sometimes problems with pieces of jewelry such as rings. If left at an angle to set, the stone may slide off the mount before the adhesive has hardened. However, there is an easy way round this. Simply keep a small bowl filled with salt or fine dry sand and stick the rings, cuff-links, etc. in this, stone side uppermost until set (see diagram 4), unless the instructions for a particular article state otherwise.

PLIERS AND TWEEZERS, (See diagram 5)

Various types of small jewelry pliers are obtainable, of which the most useful, we think, is the simple 'flat-nose' type illustrated. If you want to buy a second pair, the kind with one flat and one round 'nose' is useful, or you may occasionally find that you will need to borrow a large pair of ordinary carpenter's pliers from the family tool box. Jewelry pliers are constantly needed for opening and pinching together jump rings, pressing on bell caps, bending the claws of ring mounts, and many other jobs. A pair of tweezers, too, for fine work is very useful — so is a simple meat skewer, the thin straight, rather than the thick twisted, type. An old saucer and supply of matchsticks for mixing and applying adhesive will be needed, and some tissues for wiping off surplus glue.

Choosing mounts and stones

If you have never made any gemstone jewelry before, it can be quite bewildering to encounter for the first time the variety of mounts and stones on the counter of the lapidary's shop. Which do you buy first, the stones or the mounts? On the whole, we think it is better to start by buying a few mounts — say, two or three flat pad ring mounts, a claw and a fancy one, a few fairly large bell caps, gilt and silver, and a flat pad bracelet mount. Then you will be able to make some of the items shown in this chapter.

Having obtained these, look through the bowls of stones available and match them up to the mounts in your hand. Advice on the most suitable stones to choose will be given with details of the items we illustrate. For instance, it would be no use choosing a baroque stone for a ring if the stone had no flattish surface which could be stuck to the mount; a stone destined to become a pendant would need to have a suitable 'drop' shape with a pointed corner on which to stick the bell cap.

With all your equipment, mounts and stones to hand, you are now ready to begin this very rewarding branch of simple jewelry making. Not only are you working with stones which have beauty and are 'real', but no very advanced techniques are required by a beginner to produce something which is most attractive and wearable. Like the other jewelry in this book, children of ten or eleven who are good with their hands and interested in making things should, as well as adults, be able to achieve interesting and attractive results, given a little help and supervision. It is the exercise of your taste and discrimination which will really count in the long run.

RINGS

Let us suppose that you have chosen three types of ring mount to start with — a flat pad mount, a claw mount and a fancy mount to hold three small stones.

Flat mount

For the flat mount, you will need to look for a stone which has a flat surface which can be stuck to the mount — but not only that. The upper surface, which will be the one to show, must be free from ugly flaws and present either an attractive pattern in the stone or a good colour. It should also be a nice shape; try the stone on your finger to decide which way round would be the most flattering on the finished ring.

Now apply adhesive to the ring mount pad and to the flat surface of the stone, having first made sure that they are both clean and free from grease (see photographs A and B). Press the stone on to the mount, in the position you have previously decided upon (see photograph C), then press the ring into your

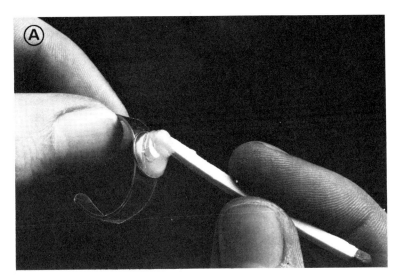

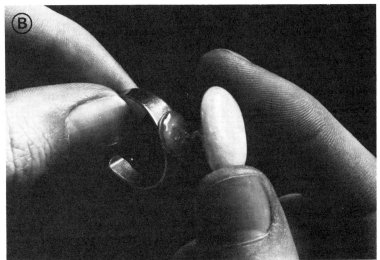

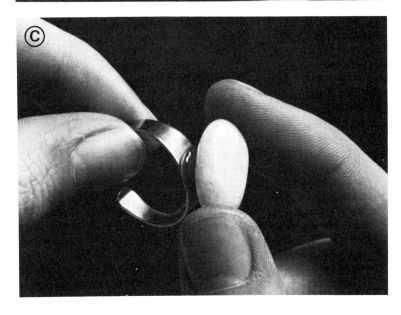

9

pot of salt or sand, with the stone uppermost and resting on the surface of the salt. Leave it in a warm place (near a radiator or the fire) to set. When the glue has hardened (leave it overnight to make sure) take out of the salt, brush off any grains that remain, and the ring is ready to wear.

Claw mount

A claw ring mount will take either a regular or irregular stone, as the claws can be bent to hold any shape. However, the claws are sometimes rather stiff to bend, and it is a good idea to work them backwards and forwards a few times with your pliers before starting to mount the stone.

Again a stone should be chosen with an attractive face surface and slightly flattened base one and its place in the mount determined by how it looks on your finger.

Place the stone in the mount and bend the claws roughly round it with your fingers. Then take it out and work on each claw with the pliers to take on the shape more accurately. Replace the stone and press each claw even more closely with the pliers until the stone is firmly surrounded. When you are satisfied with the claw position, take out the stone and apply a little adhesive to the underside and to the mount, just to make absolutely sure that it is firmly held. Replace in mount, pressing the claws again in place and leave as before for the adhesive to set.

Fancy 3-stone mount

For this type of fancy mount you will need three tiny stones, either matching in colour and type or, according to your choice, contrasting.

You will need the mount with you when choosing the stones as size can be very deceptive and you have to make sure that the stones fit well into the tiny 'cups' which hold them.

When you make the ring, you will find your tweezers useful, both for holding the stone while you apply the adhesive, and for dropping it into the setting (see photograph D). When this has been done, press each stone gently down before placing it in the salt bowl to set.

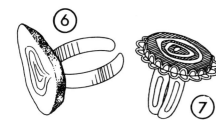

Other rings were made from a 'slice' of banded agate (see diagram 6), attractively marked, and a cabochon-cut malachite (see diagram 7), set in a gilt lace-like ring mount. In this case, and in fact anywhere where the metal shows in relation to the stone, the most flattering colour must be chosen. For instance, blue sodalite stones, turquoise, pink rose quartz, etc. generally look better with gilt mounts, whilst the browns, sands, and oranges of agates, cornelians and other quartzes are better with silver mounts. However, there are no hard and fast rules. Your own eye will quickly tell you which looks best.

PENDANTS

Once you have tried your hand at making a few rings, you will be ready to start making pendants. It is important to learn how to choose and mount pendant stones correctly on bell caps as not only will they be used to hang round the neck on a chain, but can also be made into ear rings or fixed on to bracelets too.

Whilst is it easy, with modern adhesives, to stick mount and

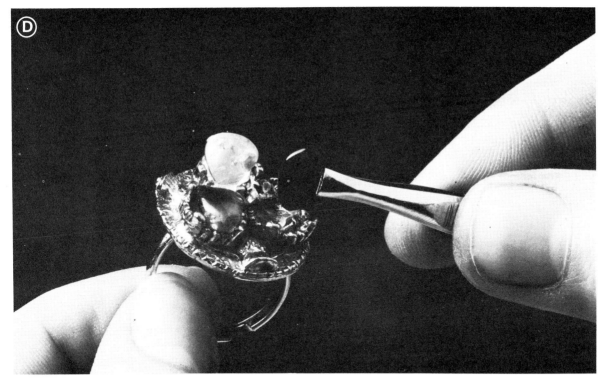

stone together, it is necessary to use some judgment and not to apply a ridiculously small bell cap to a large stone, and vice versa (see diagram 8). It would certainly not look attractive in the final result!

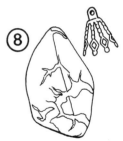

Perhaps the easiest kind to start with is the type where a suitable-shaped baroque stone with a pointed corner (not too small in size) is fixed to a fairly substantial bell cap, rather than the filigree type (see diagram 2 on p.6). When mount and stone are firmly stuck together, a jump ring is put through the small ring on the bell cap, so that the stone can be hung on a neck chain, bracelet, etc.

Choosing suitable stones and mounts

First look through a tray of stones and put on one side any attractively marked and coloured ones which are of a pleasing 'drop' shape for a pendant. Then examine these carefully, rejecting any which are too flawed or otherwise unsuitable. You will certainly find that one side of each stone will be more attractive than the other, and it will then be necessary to make your final selection on what personally appeals to you about each of the stones which is left.

When you have selected the stone, pick out a mount which will hold it comfortably and which will flatter its colour.

Making the pendant

With stone and mount in your hand, you will next have to visualise how the pendant will hang eventually on its chain or ear-ring mount, with the best or most colourful side of the stone facing outwards when it is being worn. Now press the chosen bell cap on to the stone in such a way that the eyelet is facing

you and also the best face of the stone. This means that when a jump ring is fixed through the eyelet the pendant will hang in the correct way on the chain (see diagram 9).

Make sure that the cap is pressed well down until the point of the stone touches the metal underneath the eyelet. Work the prongs round the stone, pressing them well down (see photograph E) and using the pliers to help you if necessary.

Take the cap off the stone, remembering which way you placed it, and apply a little adhesive to the point of the stone and the inside of the cap, using a matchstick. Press the cap down on to the stone as it was before and place it to set in your salt pot.

When it is quite set, open a jump ring of a suitable size, pass it through the eyelet hole on the bell cap and close the ends of the jump ring with the pliers.

Other types of pendant

The pendants described above made from baroque stones and bell caps are the most common type. but it is also possible to make other kinds from gemstones. Sometimes you will find that the lapidary sells pre-shaped stones with holes pierced to take a mount (such as the green pendant in our colour picture) or you can buy flat mounts in various shapes — heart, cross, disc, etc. — on which a stone can be stuck. For a flat 'slice' of stone, a leaf-shaped mount, which is bent over to form a hanging loop is the best kind. Photograph F shows this type of pendant being worn and you will see the same pendant in colour on the cover of the book. These slices of stone (in this case agate) are rather more expensive than the ordinary tumbled baroque stones, but are very attractive in use.

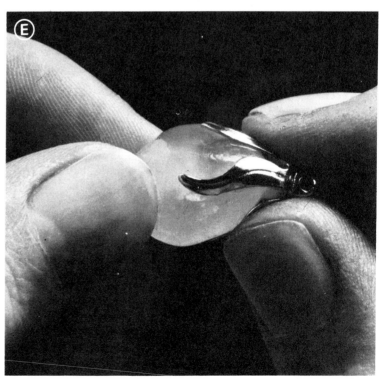

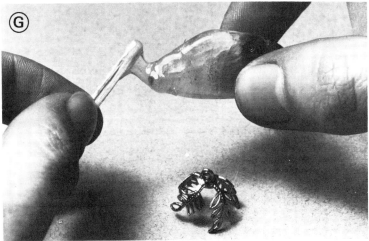

As you become more adept at making pendants you will, of course, want to experiment with differently shaped stones and mounts. Illustrated here is a large irregular stone which is being mounted on a big filigree bell cap (see photograph G), quite suitable for holding it. The dark blue of the sodalite stone is flattered by the gilt bell cap and will be hung eventually on a gilt chain.

EAR-RINGS
Having learnt to make flat-mount rings and pendants, you will now be able to try your hand at ear-rings. If you look at the mounts on p.6 you will see that several types are available,

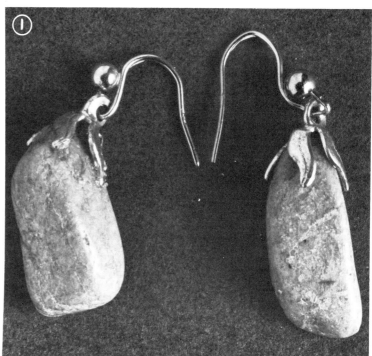

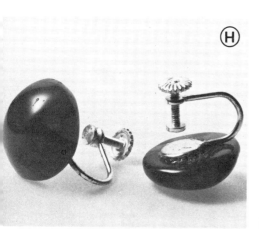

both for pierced and unpierced ears. However, there are really only two techniques as far as the stones themselves are concerned. Either a suitably-shaped stone is stuck on a flat mount, as illustrated on this page in photograph H, or a pendant stone is hung from an ear-ring mount.

Care must be taken over choosing the stones for ear-rings so that they match adequately in colour and shape and this will entail some searching through the stone trays. A well-matched pair of drop ear-rings is shown in photograph I.

Make sure that the stones are completely set in their mounts before wearing the ear-rings or they will be liable to come unstuck as they are subjected to quite heavy wear while being put on and taken off.

BRACELETS

Three attractive bracelets are shown in the colour picture and well illustrate the three most popular types of mount. (see diagram 2 on p.6).

The turquoise drop bracelet (see diagram 10) was made to match the pendant ear-rings, and the same bell cap mounts were used. Each little pendant was fixed to the bracelet chain with a gilt jump ring. It is necessary to count the number of links in the chain and space out the pendants evenly, in order to achieve a professional effect.

The bracelet round the neck of the model in the colour photograph shows the pads of the bracelet mount used as a 'frame' round each stone. These were matched in colour and roughly in shape and set exactly in the centre of the pads (see diagram 11).

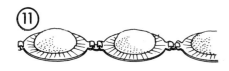

The third bracelet, lying in front of the model, illustrates the type where the pads are completely covered by the stones. In this case, another effect was tried — that of using stones of the same size and type but in different colours, graded within the same colour range (see diagram 12).

Of course, there are many variations and combinations of stones and colours possible, but these three ideas can be copied if you are a beginner.

Other types of bracelet mount are available in some shops. For instance, wide metal bands with applied metal plaques of different shapes on which handsome 'specimen' stones can be mounted.

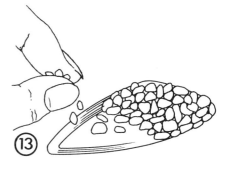

BROOCHES

As you will see from the sketches, there are two main categories of brooch mount. In the first type, the mount is simply a bar or disc of metal bearing a pin, and on this disc is stuck a stone or stones. The mount itself is completely covered.

The second type of mount, however, plays its part in the finished effect of the brooch. It is designed to show a decorative shape or setting for the stones which it displays (see photograph J). It may be recessed, so that it can be coated with adhesive and small stones or pebble chippings stuck to it (see diagram 13), or perhaps shaped to form a leaf and flower design, into which small stones can be placed. In this case, when the adhesive has been placed on the mount and stones, the brooch should be left right way up to dry in the salt bowl. In this way it can be kept level.

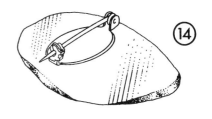

If however, you are using the first type of mount, that is, where a large stone is stuck to a flat metal pad, the stone should be pressed lightly down into the salt and the mount should be pin upwards (see diagram 14). If the stone is irregular in shape you must first, of course, plan the position of the mount, so that when pinned on a dress or coat the stone is the right way up. A simple but attractive brooch of this kind, made from a single well-marked brown agate is shown in the colour picture, just in front of the model.

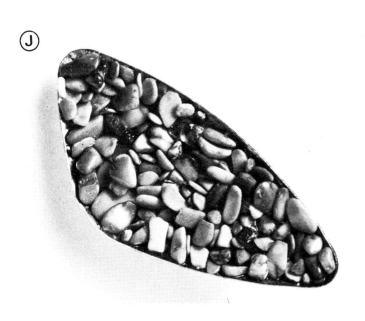

MEN'S JEWELRY

Gemstones lend themselves very well to making such things as cuff-links, tie clips, key rings and so on, and the subdued colours of some of the agates and quartzes would be acceptable to the most conservative of men. However, if his taste in colour and jewels is more flamboyant, there are plenty of stones to satisfy this, too.

Cuff links

These mounts are available in a variety of types, with links, solid or wide chain fastenings, and they may have a flat pad for mounting the stone, or a recessed one which will take a shaped cabochon stone.

If you decide on a cabochon stone in a recessed mount (and as cuff links take a good deal of wear you may feel that this is worth the cost of the more expensive stones) make sure that the stone is the correct size grade. They vary considerably, but are standardised in sizing and the assistant will show you the correct tray to choose from. Again the mount and stone should be coated with adhesive and, when put together, pressed in salt to set. Be sure to allow the maximum 'curing' time for the

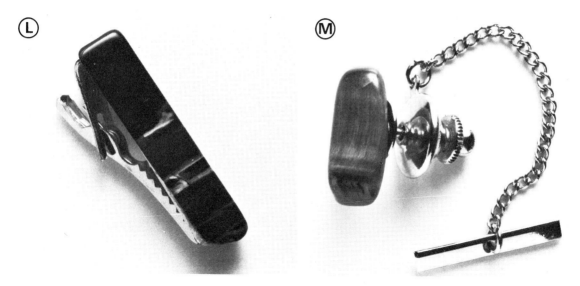

L

M

adhesives before using the cuff links so that the stones are as firmly set in as possible.

For flat pad mounts, choose a pair of matching baroque stones, each with a good flat sticking surface. They should be roughly the same in shape, colour and marking so you may have a long search before finding just the right pair. If you are making links to be worn with a business suit, such stones as tiger's eye or Mexican crazy lace agate (as illustrated in photograph K) would be very suitable. Again make sure that plenty of adhesive is used and the stones very firmly stuck before they are put to use.

Tie pins

Tie pins are not a very easy shape to work with, as the mount itself is long and narrow and the finished effect on the tie should be the same. You can either mount one to three small stones on the bar and leave some of the metal showing, or try to find the odd long shaped stone which would fit. The one shown in photograph L is made from a piece of banded agate cut into a triangular shape, and by a lucky chance it was of just the right length for the mount as you will see from the illustration.

Tie tacks

These are easier to make than tie clips as the mount simply takes one small stone (see photograph M). To add interest for the recipient of the gift, you might make it from his birth stone – check on the semi-precious equivalent of his precious stone birth gem. The shop where you buy your stones should have a list.

Key rings

A welcome present for both men and women and you will need a large, handsome stone suitable for using with a strong bell cap. Mount the stone as if you were making a pendant and attach it to a key ring mount using a strong jump ring. Again it is important not to subject the key ring to hard wear until the adhesive has completely set.

2. Orange Peel Jewelry

The title of this chapter may well make you rub your eyes and wonder if you've read the words correctly, but yes! jewelry really can be made out of orange peel, if you know how — and we are grateful to the Outspan organisation for the original idea.

It's a particularly good craft for children as orange peel is easy to work with, apart from paint and mounts the basic material costs nothing (you'd normally throw it away, wouldn't you?), and they can mystify their friends with the results. Out of eight people we asked to identify the material this finished jewelry was made from. not one guessed correctly!

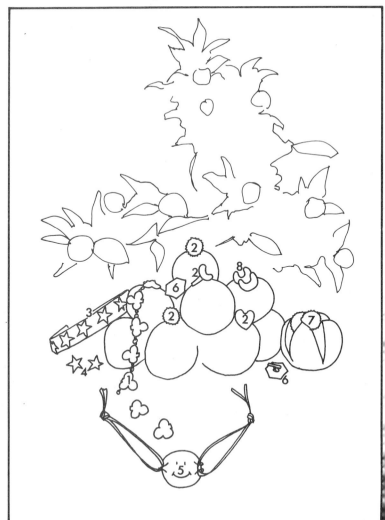

Key to colour picture
1. Shamrock bracelet
2. 'Pop Art' rings
3. Starry headband
4. Star ear rings
5. 'Smiley' wrist band
6. Cuff links
7. Double circle brooch
8. Half moon ear rings

When it is just peeled from the fruit, orange peel is very easy to cut with knife, scissors, pastry cutters or even the edge of a glass. And it can be perforated easily using a skewer or, if you have one, a leather punch. If the cut-out shapes are spread out on a tray and left for five or six days in the airing cupboard to dry out gradually, they will acquire the texture of firm leather. The natural colour will have darkened during drying and become a very pleasant 'burnt orange'; but, in fact, the skin takes paint very well — either metallic or plain colours. In the jewelry illustrated, we used plastic enamel paints, available in small phials. These are intermixable so that you can make subtle colours as well as using the straight primary ones. The orange side, when painted, has an attractive grainy texture.

Materials needed

As it takes the peel shapes up to a week to dry out, it is a good idea to plan several pieces of jewelry at once and cut out the shapes at the same time. This means that the family must be resigned to a large quantity of orange juice and orange compôte for a few days! So the first thing you will need is plenty of peel. Choose oranges with medium thick peel; if it is too thin, the shapes will warp too much in the drying, if it is too thick the shapes will look clumsy. Peel the orange neatly in quarters using a sharp knife (see diagram 1). Make sure that all the flesh comes away leaving clean whole quarters.

You will also need, for the jewelry we suggest making, a set of miniature pastry cutters in different shapes (see diagram 2), a metal skewer, scissors, plastic enamel paints of different colours, small tins of metallic paint and one of clear enamel (the kind used in model making), a small paint brush, some white spirit (for cleaning the brush) and a supply of paper tissues. To mount the jewelry you will need a supply of mounts, jump rings and epoxy resin adhesive of the types suggested in chapter 1. Exactly what you will need will be given in the directions for making each piece of jewelry. In some cases, leather thonging will be required.

General hints on making the jewelry

As previously mentioned, the peel should be dried in the warm atmosphere of the airing cupboard. There is no point in trying to dry it out more quickly by putting it in the oven — it will only become brittle and crack. Nor should it be left in a damp place, or mould will form on it.

However ideal the drying conditions, you will almost certainly find that a few of each shape will have to be thrown away for some reason, because they have cracked or warped too much, or simply because you have damaged them in the mounting. Therefore it pays to make several extra shapes for each piece of jewelry.

Remember, too, that if the jewelry requires pierced holes in the peel it is much easier to make them when the peel is still soft. If you forget, you will have to drill the shape and run the risk of cracking it.

Another thing to bear in mind is that considerable shrinkage takes place when the peel dries. You will see from the accompanying illustration (photograph A) how much smaller the

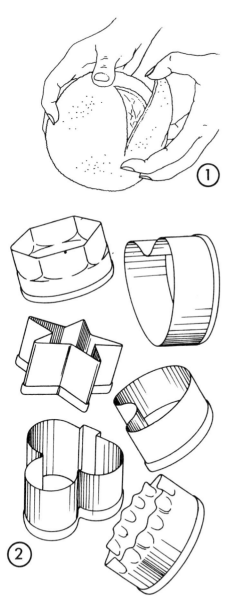

finished shape is when it is dry than when it was first cut. So if you are planning, say, a belt or bracelet which needs a number of shapes to complete it, allow for shrinkage in your measurements.

Here are some ideas for you to make.

SHAMROCK BRACELET
You will need: A miniature cutter shaped like a shamrock or clover leaf and sufficient orange peel to cut out eight or nine leaves (you will, in fact, need only six or seven for the bracelet, according to the size of your wrist; the rest are spares to allow for spoiling, or two of them can be used to make matching ear-rings); seven or eight gilt jump rings, large size, and a gilt spring fastening; green and copper plastic enamel paints and a fine brush; skewer.

To make the bracelet: Cut out eight or nine leaf shapes with the cutter and leave to dry as previously instructed, having first pierced a hole with the skewer in the edge of each of the side leaves.

When the peel has dried, pick out the six or seven shapes which have dried flattest and paint the orange surface with green enamel (see diagram 3). When dry, paint the edges and undersides of the leaves with copper paint.

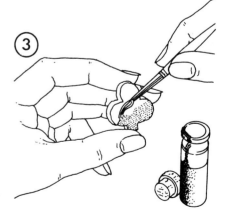

Now run the skewer into each of the pierced holes to clear them of any peel fragments or paint, and attach them together in a row stems facing alternate ways, copper sides down, using large gilt jump rings (see photograph B). Measure your wrist when you have a row of six; if this is not long enough to go round, add another leaf. The leaf at one end of the row should have a jump ring and the leaf at the other a jump ring and the spring fastening, to complete the bracelet.

'POP ART' RINGS
A great variety of pretty rings can be made from orange peel shapes, painted in all the patterns your ingenuity can devise, and

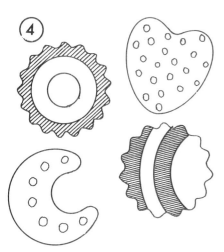

simply stuck to flat pad ring mounts with adhesive. In diagram 4 we show four of them and give the colours for painting them. They were all cut with miniature cutters.

Heart: Cut and dry a heart shape and, when dry, paint front and back with red paint. Allow paint to dry and then dot the side which shows with small silver spots. Stick on a ring mount and leave to set.

Pop circle (1): Cut a serrated-edge circle and allow to dry. Paint a yellow disc in the centre, surround with a green circle, then a blue circle and paint the edge of the shape and the back green. Each colour should be allowed to dry before applying the next one. Stick on a ring mount as above.

Pop circle (2): Cut a shape as above, and paint the back and edge black. Paint the front of the circle in curved stripes, starting with yellow, then blue, then black — and leave the last segment the natural orange colour. Allow to dry between each colour, then varnish over with clear varnish. Mount as above.

Lucky horseshoe ring: Cut out a half-moon or horseshoe shape with the appropriate cutter and leave to dry. Paint back and edge black and the front gold. Mix together a little blue and

Key to colour picture

1. Claw ring
2. 3-stone ring
3. Banded agate ring
4. Cabochon cut malachite ring
5. Sodalite pendant
6. Preformed pierced pendant
7. Turquoise pendant ear rings
8. Green serpentine pendant ear rings
9. Carnelian flat-mount ear rings
10. Turquoise pendant bracelet
11. Bracelet with decorative mount
12. Flat-pad agate bracelet
13. Agate brooch
14. Tie clip

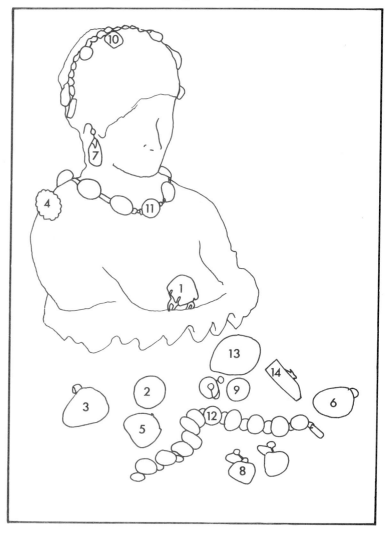

red paint to form a purple and paint large spots at intervals along the gold surface. Mount on a gilt ring mount, either with the points of the 'horseshoe' upwards or pointing to one side.

Any of the first three shapes can also be used to make brooches, simply by sticking them to brooch mounts rather than to ring mounts.

STARRY HEADBAND

One of the most attractive shapes available in small pastry cutters is the star shape. We used it to make a '7-star' headband and matching ear-rings (see photograph C). Another way of mounting the stars is shown on p. 28.

First cut out twelve star shapes — seven for the headband, two for the ear-rings and three 'spares'. Allow to dry.

Paint all the stars with copper paint on the top surface and with dark blue paint on the edges and under surfaces.

Buy a stiff headband at a chain store — almost any kind will do as you can always paint it if the colour is not attractive. We used a stiff band covered with black 'leather'. Arrange seven of the stars in a row along the top part of the band and mark the positions with a pencil mark. Put a dot of adhesive on these marks and coat the back surfaces of the stars with adhesive. As these are being stuck on a curved surface they will be liable to slip, so it is advisable to allow the adhesive to set slightly and become 'tacky' before sticking the stars on to the band. Each leg of the band can be pressed into a salt pot (see diagram 5) whilst the stars are setting, or it can be hung over a glass or jar so the band can be kept upright. Stick two of the stars on small ear-ring mounts and press into the salt pot to set.

'SMILEY' WRIST BAND

Smiley, the jolly face with the big smile, has been with us for some time and he's easy to copy on an orange peel disc. There's no need to choose *his* face if you don't want to — you can copy Mickey Mouse, Goofy or any current favourite instead.

You will need a large piece of orange peel, some copper wire

24

and two lengths of leather thonging, each about ten inches long, some yellow and some black paint. (Alternatively you can draw his features with a black felt tip pen and varnish over).

Cut out one or two pieces of peel using a small glass as a cutter. We used one with a diameter of $2\frac{1}{2}$ ins. Leave to dry, having first pierced two holes on each side of the disc with your skewer.

Select the best and flattest piece when dry, and paint on both sides with yellow paint. Leave to dry. When quite dry, paint in black with a fine brush or use a black felt tip pen to mark on the Smiley features. Varnish over with clear varnish when dry.

Cut short lengths of copper wire, thread through the four holes and bend round to form circles. Thread a length of thonging through each and tie in a knot (see diagram 6). Get a friend to tie the band round your wrist. You could, of course, make the lengths of thonging longer and wear the Smiley as a choker.

CLEOPATRA NECKLACE

For this dramatic necklace (see photograph D), you will need plenty of peel to give you twenty-one discs $1\frac{1}{2}$ ins. in diameter, with a few extras. Again, a small glass can serve as a cutter, or use a small pastry cutter if you have one the correct size.

When the discs are stamped out, pierce four holes in each,

at equal intervals round the rim to take the joining wires. Leave one or two discs with only two pierced holes for the bottom point of the necklace. You will also need, for this necklace, a chain with large links to fit closely round your neck, a quantity of large and medium jump rings, either gold or silver to match the neck chain, and paint in any colour you choose (we think gold or silver looks best for this particular necklace, but of course it need not be either of these).

When the peel has dried, paint it on both sides in the chosen paint and allow to dry. Now fit a large jump ring through each hole, except on the bottom disc which will only need two rings. Join the discs together by passing a small jump ring through adjoining large rings as shown in the photograph, working so that you form an inverted cone shape.

Attach the top row to the chain to give the finished effect as shown.

Another effect with stars

An alternative to the star headband on p.24 is the star choker shown here in photograph F. Five stars are used, joined

Key to colour picture

1. Ear rings from 'Aristotle's lanterns'
2. Heart cockle pendant
3. Shell section pendant
4. Shell section ear rings
5. Shell section bracelet
6. Sundial shell ring
7. Pendant from rose petal tellin shells
8. Ring to match 7
9. Shell and pebble butterfly brooch
10. 'Victorian' shell brooch
11. Ear ring to match 10

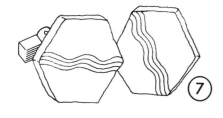

together with jump rings in the same way as the disc above (holes should be pierced in two points of each star as shown, before drying and painting).

When the stars are linked together, they can be stitched through three of the jump rings to a velvet band. Measure the size to fit your neck, and finish the ends of the band with pieces of Velcro fastening.

Matching ear rings can be made by sticking a star in the centre of a plain flat ear ring the same colour as the ribbon band.

CUFF LINKS

These can look much more expensive than they really are and provide quite a talking point at lunch time!

We used a miniature hexagonal pastry cutter for the three shapes we cut. When dried, the chosen two were painted gold on the underside of the peel, to see how the texture compared with painting on the orange side. In fact, the texture is very pleasant, and smoother than the orange side (see diagram 7).

When the gold paint was dry, a thick wavy line was drawn across each shape as shown, using brown paint, and after drying, a thin silver line was drawn down the centre of this line, following its curves.

The orange side of the peel was not painted, and the mounts were stuck on this side and left to set.

BELT

Plenty of peel will be needed for the belt in photograph E, especially if you wear it as a hipster belt as the model did! You will also require three yards of leather thonging and your own colour choice of plastic enamel paint. As fairly large holes will be required for threading the thonging, you will need a thicker skewer than usual, or use a needlework stiletto or leather punch if you have one for the job.

Using a sharp knife, cut out squares of orange peel $1\frac{1}{2}$ ins. by $1\frac{1}{2}$ ins. and punch a hole in each corner. You will need approximately thirty to forty squares, depending on your own measurements. When the squares are dry, paint to your colour choice on the orange side, or leave the natural colour and paint or spray with clear varnish.

Cut the thonging in half and thread through the squares as shown in the photograph. Leave the ends long so that they can be tied and hang down.

DOUBLE RING BROOCH

This simple little brooch (diagram 8) looks attractive on a scarf or tweed suit, and it consists simply of two serrated circles of peel (cut with a miniature cutter) painted in different colours and stuck one to overlap the other. A brooch mount is then stuck on the back. We chose copper and brown for the brooch in the illustration.

HALF MOON EAR RINGS

Cut and dry three or four half moon shapes with a miniature cutter and paint the orange side with gold paint and the edge and back with black. When dry, mount on ear ring mounts, choosing the type with small pads so that they are completely covered by the half moon (see diagram 9).

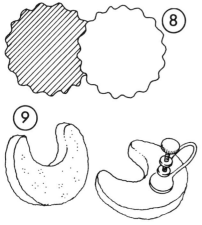

3. Shell Jewelry

(See colour photograph on p.27)

Like gemstone jewelry, shell jewelry has a fascination all its own — the delight of working with something 'real' rather than something manufactured (see photograph A). The Victorians had a great feeling for shells and delighted to use them for covering trinket boxes, framing mirrors, pictures and seaside souvenirs, and of course for jewelry. The craft of shell work is enjoying a revival, and with modern glues it is easy to create lovely jewelry even from fragile-looking specimens.

You can, of course, collect your own shells on visits to the seaside, or, if you live far from the sea, it is usually possible to find a specialist shell shop or craft shop which sells bags of assorted specimens as well as more expensive and exotic single ones. You can also buy 'sliced' shells, which can give some exquisite effects as we shall show in this chapter.

You will find that your shell jewelry will fall into one of two types. In the first, Nature has done most of the work for you· and has formed a perfect jewel which needs only the simplest of mounts to enable it to be worn. In the second, you can use what Nature provides and form it into patterns and arrangements before turning it into something you can wear.

On the whole, we think that shell jewelry is best in the natural colours in which the shells are found, but you can obtain dyed ones if you want them, or paint or tint your own.

One piece of equipment you will need is patience — plenty of it, as the small shells used for some of the jewelry shown here need a great deal of manoeuvring into position and once there, must be coaxed to stick with some care. Also, it can be tricky balancing a mount or finding until it has stuck — although once the adhesive has set firmly, the mount will stay well in place.

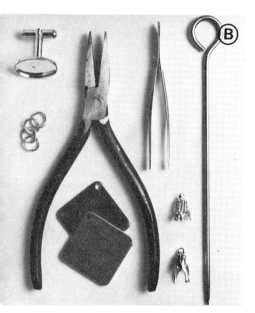

Equipment needed   *(see photograph B)*

You will require some flat copper mounts — the kind used for enamelling — as a basis for some of the jewelry shown in this chapter. We give shapes and sizes separately, and if you go on making shell jewelry, it is a good idea to keep a few of these mounts in stock. Very often the shape will suggest a design you can make, after you have bought or collected a new selection of shells. For instance, the shell butterfly brooch in the colour picture almost designed itself. The circular mount was there, the ordinary little white shells were found to have naturally tinted purple interiors and were the shapes of butterfly wings, and what could be more like a butterfly's body than the spiral, graceful auger shell?

You will also need adhesive (see Gemstone chapter), your pliers, tweezers for moving and adjusting small shells, mounts and findings such as bell caps, jump rings, etc. and a skewer is also useful at times.

Study this chapter before actually going out to buy shells so that if there is anything you particularly want to copy, you will know what to ask for.

Key to colour picture
1. Fish key ring
2. Flower belt fob
3. Oval 'heart-throb' pendant
4. Sea horse ear rings
5. Copper chippings ring
6. Copper chippings ornament
7. Cuff links from watch parts
8. Ring from watch works
9. Sequin pendant
10. Holiday souvenir belt ornament

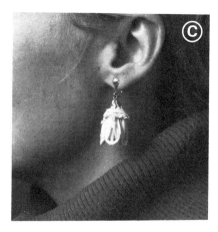

OLD IVORY EAR RINGS

The exquisite drop ear rings shown in photograph C were made from just two shells (or, to be strictly accurate, the mandibles of the sea urchin!) – 'Aristotle's lanterns'. They have the colour and delicacy of old ivory, but in fact are not really very fragile. They are particularly suited to mounting on bell caps as there is a naturally raised part at the top on to which these can be stuck. For creamy coloured shells, gold mounts are the obvious choice, and the two plain gilt bell caps and gilt ear ring mounts set off the shells perfectly.

To make the ear rings: Take each shell and apply a little adhesive to the projecting part at the top. Apply adhesive also to the interior of the bell cap. You will find that there is no need to open the claws of the bell cap to any great extent before mounting on the shell (see diagram 1).

Press the bell caps on the shells and leave until the adhesive is completely set. Then hang on the ear ring mounts and squeeze the mounting ring closed with your jewelry pliers

OLD IVORY HEART PENDANT

It's hard to believe that the perfect ivory heart shown on the model in photograph D is really a natural shell – but it is, in fact, a heart cockle. It opens naturally from the point of the heart to the top and, before mounting it, it is advisable to prise the edges of the split gently apart and apply a little adhesive, closing it and allowing it to stick so that the shell is a firm and complete 'unit'.

When you have done this and the adhesive is set, a jump ring can be stuck on to form the shell into a pendant. This is not particularly easy as the ring must be opened just the right amount to slip on the shell and it is necessary to keep adjusting it with the pliers. If you try to open it by pressing it on the shell, you will end by breaking the shell itself. Diagram 2 on this page shows how the ring should be placed.

When the ring is opened to the right size, apply adhesive to the ends and also to the shell, and wait a little while for it to become tacky. Then press the shell point down in the salt pot and apply the ring, using your tweezers and, if necessary, the skewer to adjust it.

The ring should now set in the correct position, but it is advisable to leave it for the full 'curing' time of the adhesive before hanging on a chain and wearing. As you will see, the ring is facing the right way for hanging without using a further jump ring.

JEWELRY FROM SHELL SECTIONS

We have made up several examples of the kind of jewelry you can make from ready-prepared shell sections. Of course, you may not be able to buy exactly similar sections from your local shop, but you can adapt what it has to offer after studying the examples on these pages.

PENDANT

A section cut from a conch shell makes a handsome pendant. Again it is kept in its natural colours – cream, with a faint tinge of orange in the convolutions. You will find that such sections have two different 'faces' and you can choose which is the more attractive when you are mounting it.

It is necessary when putting on the bell cap to make sure that the prongs of the cap are so placed that they do not spoil the basic shape of the shell, so experiment carefully with cap and shell before applying any adhesive (see photograph E). See that the small ring on the cap is facing the same way as the front face of the shell, too, when you arrange the prongs.

When you are satisfied with the appearance of shell and cap, apply adhesive to both and leave to set in the salt pot. When quite dry, run a jump ring through the ring on the cap so that the finished pendant may be hung on a chain.

EAR-RINGS

The small white volute shell sections shown in the colour picture were mounted in a similar way to the pendant above, but using much smaller filigree mounts (see photograph F). They were then hung on ear-ring screw mounts, care being taken that each shell curved inwards.

BRACELET

The bracelet shown in the colour photograph is made from yet another type of shell section. As many of the mounted sections as you like may be hung from a chain, arranged in any way you fancy.

As with the heart pendant, it is not very easy to apply a mount to these shells. Again, the best way is to use a jump ring opened up so that the points enclose the top part of the shell section (see diagram 3). Apply adhesive both to the points of the ring and to the shell and allow to become tacky before sticking together and leaving in the salt pot to set.

When completely dry (leave for the maximum period of 'curing' time), pass another jump ring through the first and attach this to a suitable chain.

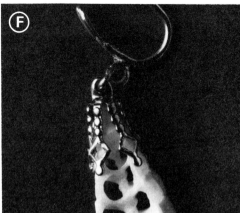

SIMPLE LITTLE RING

The little ring shown in photograph G is very simply made by sticking a small variegated sundial shell to a thin silver ring mount. Do, however, make sure you choose a shell which is unusual or attractive in its colours and markings. You can vary the idea by using, perhaps, winkle shells, well cleaned and either varnished or painted with a colour or with a metallic paint. If using a winkle shell, it is advisable to fill the opening (this is the side which will be stuck to the mount) with a little clay, plastic wood or similar substance as the opening is rather large and there should be a good surface to stick on to the mount.

PINK SHELL PENDANT

We now come to some rather more complicated pieces made with small rose petal tellin shells, starting with the pink heart pendant shown in photograph H.

The basis for the pendant was a heart-shaped copper mount, pierced at the centre top with a hole to allow for hanging it, but of course any shaped mount would be suitable. Before starting work, make a preliminary selection from a heap of shells – choosing only perfect specimens and those with a good strong colour.

Coat the front of the mount with a thin layer of adhesive or clear varnish and place a perfectly shaped shell face downwards in the middle. It is from this shell that the others will radiate. Next arrange round it a row of shells, point downward and curving inwards like the petals of a flower. To get each shell to remain upright, you will have to push a shell placed flat and face down behind it to hold it in position (see diagram 4). Use a skewer to do this, and keep wiping the point free of glue or varnish or the shells will stick to it. Continue to build up the rows of upright and flat shells in the same way until you have filled up your mount shape. Leave to set, then fix a jump ring through the hole at the top so that the pendant may be hung.

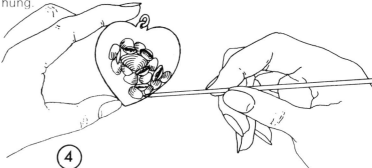

You will find that the metal of the mount will show a little between the shells and can completely change their colour. A gold or copper mount will make pink shells appear a more intense pink, but if you use a silver mount, pink shells will take on a violet or mauve tint.

PINK SHELL RING

You can make a pretty ring to match the pendant above (see photograph), using a recessed ring mount (the kind intended for mounting a cabochon cut stone) and the same small pink shells. Build them upright in concentric circles to form a rose or

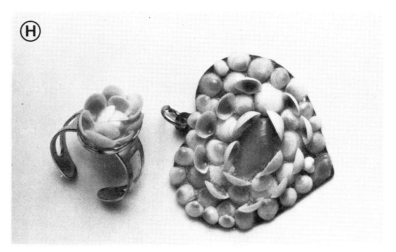

flower shape as shown in diagram 5 — there is no room in this small mount to place a shell flat in the middle. As before, glue or varnish may be used. Alternatively, make matching cuff-links with a similarly recessed mount.

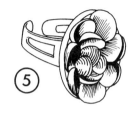

BUTTERFLY BROOCH

The pretty butterfly brooch was built up from shells and pebble chippings, all in their natural colours (see photograph I on this page).

To copy, plan out your design on the mount before applying any adhesive, to make sure that you get the shells in the right positions and the right proportions. When you are satisfied with the design, remove the shells and put aside in roughly the same position as you will want to use them. Now coat the mount with a layer of varnish or adhesive and stick the graceful auger, the body, shell and the pearly trochus head in place. Next position the top two wings (tiny clam shells), then the lower two and press in position (see diagram 6). Fill in the empty space at the top of the mount with a layer of pebble chippings and the lower part with tiny pink shells, convex side up. Stick two of the same shells on the upper wings, concave side up, as shown. Press the brooch, pin side down, in the salt pot to dry.

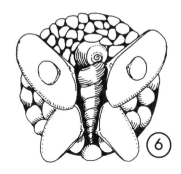

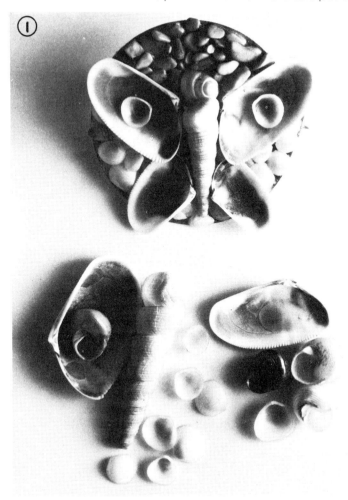

'VICTORIAN' BROOCH AND EAR RINGS

Although they may look complicated to copy, the white and purple Victorian-type brooch and ear rings shown on this page in photograph J, are not too difficult to copy. In fact, they are made up of only three different types of shell, sections such as the ones used for the bracelet (but smaller), pearly trochus and tiny white margin shells (see diagram 7).

In this case, the inside of the shell sections was painted with plastic enamel paint to give some colour to an otherwise completely white arrangement.

To make the set, you will need a flat oval metal mount and two small round metal mounts, a brooch pin mount and two screw-on ear ring mounts. You will also require adhesive and your pliers and skewer for working with.

Start first with the oval brooch mount as this is larger and therefore easier to work with. Coat one side of the mount with adhesive and, in the centre, stick a margin shell on end pointing up, holding it in place on each side with a section shell placed as shown in the photograph. On each side of these stick two more sections, then beyond them two more open sections, projecting beyond the rim of the mount.

Stick two more open sections on the long edges of the mount, facing each other. Placing is shown in photograph J.

Now place the other margin shells in position, and finally the pearly trochus shells. As some of the latter overlap the margin shells, you will need to apply a little more adhesive to stick them firmly.

When the shells are firmly stuck to the mount, paint the insides of the shell sections with your chosen colour, then stick the complete arrangement on a brooch mount and leave in the salt pot to set.

Make two smaller arrangements on the flat round mounts for ear-rings. You will only require two shell sections (again tinted like the ones in the brooch), one pearly trochus and two margin shells. Stick down in a similar way, and when quite set, mount on the ear-ring mounts (see diagram 8).

You will notice that on the brooch the margin shells are in two sizes, one being very small. If you have difficulty in obtaining these, you could use tiny branches of coral instead. In fact, of course, once you have the idea, you can try any suitable combination of shells to make similar more elaborate brooches.

4. Jewelry From Plastic Settings

(See colour photograph on p.31)

For this branch of jewelry making, you will first be making the 'jewel' yourself – a rather time-consuming, but very satisfying and interesting exercise!

Essentially, the idea is to set interesting objects, whether made or natural, in a clear solid plastic, and then mount them as pieces of jewelry. First of all, then it is necessary to learn how to do the embedding, which requires some care until you become practised.

You will need

1. A supply of liquid plastic and hardener, which works on the same principle as the epoxy resin adhesive described in chapter 1. The type under the trade name of Plasticraft is widely available in the U.K.
2. A set of moulds of different shapes and sizes for setting the objects (see diagram 1). These are obtainable made in plastic or pottery, or you can use a suitably shaped cup or basin, or even a tin, such as a self-adhesive tape tin.
3. A marked measuring cup – these are usually available at the shop where you buy your liquid plastic – and cocktail sticks or something similar for mixing the plastic (see diagram 2).
4. Mould release wax (again sold where you buy your plastic). This is needed to enable the setting to be removed more easily from the mould.
5. Colouring agent or plastic enamel paint for 'backing' the setting if necessary.
6. The finest grade of wet and dry sandpaper.
7. Tweezers and skewer or cocktail stick for handling and moving the objects to be set.
8. Something to set. The number and variety of things which can be set is infinite – we suggest just a very few in this chapter, from a butterfly, shells, photograph, fish, watch

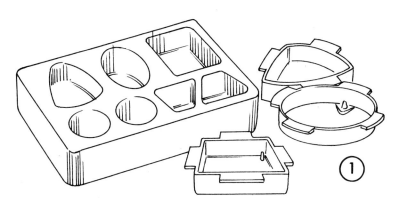

parts, copper chippings, sequins, holiday souvenirs such as stamps, coins, etc. etc. By experimenting you will soon find which types of material you most enjoy working with and how you can obtain the best effects.

Although there should be an instruction leaflet with your bottle of plastic and hardener, it can easily be mislaid, so for future reference we will run through here the method of setting articles and releasing castings from the mould.

Preparing the mould

First wipe the mould round with a clean tissue, then rub round it with a little mould release wax. Leave for a few minutes to allow the wax to dry, then polish with a clean dry cloth or clean paper tissue. Repeat this process once again, making sure that there are no lumps of wax left in the corners of the mould as these will show on the finished casting. The mould is now ready to use.

First layer of plastic

Measure out 10 ml. of liquid plastic in the measuring cup and add 5 drops of hardener (these are the proportions you should always use when mixing larger quantities for big settings later on).

Stir the mixture thoroughly then pour a little into the prepared mould shape so that the bottom surface is just covered. Place the mould in a warm place on a level surface and leave to set until the plastic does not move when the mould is tilted slightly. This should take from twenty minutes to an hour, depending how warm the room is. If there is any plastic left in the measuring cup, wipe it out with a paper tissue as it, too, will set if left and you will want to use the measuring cup again for the next stage.

Embedding the object to be set

First prepare a quantity of plastic and hardener in the proportions given above, mixing the amount you think you will require to fill the mould or give the depth needed if this is shallower than the complete depth of the mould.

Place the object to be embedded on top of the set layer of plastic, face down. Pour the liquid plastic over the object so that it is completely covered. If it has a flat surface facing down, move it about using a skewer or your tweezers to make sure that no air bubble is trapped underneath. If the object is likely to float (this may happen if it is something light such as an insect, sea horse, flower, etc.) pour only a little liquid plastic over it at first to stick it down, and allow this to set before covering with the deeper layer of plastic.

If you want to set one lot of objects behind another (for instance, watch parts) build up thin layers of plastic, each containing some of the things to be set.

Again place the mould in a warm place on a level surface and leave for at least an hour or until the plastic is firm. Do not place the mould on a radiator or in the oven —if setting takes place too quickly the surface of the plastic is likely to dry with wrinkles in it.

You can now either leave the casting to set completely (see

below) or finish with a third layer of coloured plastic to make a backing. If you want to add a coloured layer, work as follows. Pour 5 ml. of liquid plastic into a mixing dish and add a small quantity of colour pigment on the end of a cocktail stick or match stick, stirring very thoroughly. Add ten drops of hardener and stir into the coloured liquid plastic (the extra quantity of hardener is needed because of the colour). Completely cover the second layer of the casting with the coloured liquid plastic and leave overnight in a warm place to set.

Removing the casting from the mould

This process requires your attention, for forty minutes or so. First immerse the mould completely in boiling or very hot water for ten minutes. Next immerse the mould *upside down* in very cold water for ten minutes. Repeat these processes again. The casting should then drop easily from the mould (see photograph A). If there is difficulty in getting it to do so, a few taps on the mould should do the trick.

To finish the casting

An ordinary medium sandpaper may be used to rub down the back surface of the casting, or use the sanding attachment on a power drill. However, for jewelry a better finish is obtained by rubbing the back with the very finest grade of wet and dry sandpaper, used wet. When rubbed down, wipe dry and finish with a coat of clear varnish or nail varnish.

Some snags you may encounter

When using a new material for the first time, a few difficulties may arise and it is as well to know what they are so that they can be avoided as far as possible.

(A)

First make sure you use the liquid plastic within six months of buying it, otherwise it will get too thick to make good castings. Unless you are intending to make large quantities of jewelry, it is better to buy the smaller size bottles of plastic so that it is used up in a short space of time. Store the plastic in a cool place and use in a well-ventilated room. It is inflammable when liquid, so keep away from a naked flame.

Always make sure not to scratch or chip your moulds as these marks will show on the surface of your casting, and be sure to polish out all unevenness in the mould release wax before casting for the same reason.

If you have very great difficulty in releasing the casting from the mould it may be that the mould was not fully waxed or the casting has not set completely. Ease the casting from side to side by pushing the back surface with your thumbs and tap the mould to release, as advised above.

Never use coloured pigment in the measuring cup as it is difficult to wash out. If you have difficulty in cleaning out the clear plastic surplus so that the cup can be used again, wash it out with detergent and water.

If the colour layer, when looked at from the front of the casting, does not appear smooth and even, it will probably mean that the colouring pigment has not been mixed well enough with the liquid plastic, or that the colour layer has been poured on before the layer underneath has had time to set sufficiently.

Following the instructions above, you should now be able to make some beautiful and attractive jewelry. The instructions on the following pages will give you a selection of ideas to start you off.

FISH KEY RING

The casting containing a fish and 'coral' in our photograph B was mounted on a key ring mount, but could have easily formed a pendant or belt fob. A dead bee or other attractive insect could also be used. To make it, work as follows.

You will need a small dried fish and a piece of dried grass dyed orange. There is no need to stick to the kind we used as long as they look attractive when arranged together and are the right size for the mould you use. We chose an oval one, about one inch deep.

First wax the mould as described above, then mix together the suggested quantity of plastic and hardener, pouring a little (about $\frac{1}{8}$ inch) into the bottom of the mould. When this has partly set, after about an hour in a warm room, place the fish in position.

The fish we used was very light, so it was necessary to pour a little plastic over it to stick it in place and allow this to set before pouring over enough plastic to cover it. When this covering layer has set, embed the dried grass in the same way, remembering your original arrangement. In our case, the stem of the grass lay behind the body of the fish so that when the casting was released, it would not show on the right side.

Finally, you can back the casting with a layer of colour as previously described. We did, in fact, leave our casting clear

as we thought it looked more attractive.

When the casting has set, go through the release procedure as described, and sand down the back. Finish with a layer of clear varnish.

You are now ready to mount the casting on the key ring and the simplest way to do this without drilling it is to stick a large jump ring at the back, using adhesive and allowing it to project above the top of the casting as shown in the sketch. When the adhesive is thoroughly set for the maximum curing time, attach a key ring mount using another jump ring.

FLOWER BELT FOB

We used the same mould as for the fish setting to make an attractive belt fob (see photograph C). To copy, you will need an everlasting or artificial flower the right size to fit the mould comfortably, leaving space round it, a piece of chain so that the fob can be hung on a belt, and some turquoise chippings.

©

Wax the mould, pour in the first plastic layer and allow to set. Arrange the flower, open 'face' downwards on the plastic, setting in place with liquid plastic. When this has set, pour over more plastic, tilting the mould slightly in all directions to make sure that no air bubbles are trapped in the petals of the flower. (In some settings with flowers or leaves, you might find it looked attractive to have some bubbles on the petals — experiment, if you wish.) Leave to set.

When set, release the casting from the mould. In this case, there is no need to polish the back. Instead, paint it with varnish or a little liquid plastic and hardener and sprinkle with turquoise chippings, having attached a link of the hanging chain from the top. When set, shake off any loose chippings there may be on the surface and paint over with a further layer of varnish to hold the stones and chain more securely. Allow to dry thoroughly before hanging the fob on a narrow chain or rouleau belt.

OVAL 'HEART-THROB' PENDANT

Another way to use the oval mould is to make a pendant containing a photograph which is framed with an attractive surround such as plaited hair, gold beads or shells, as in our photograph. When worn as a pendant, these castings look better if they are shallower than the ones we have already described, and, in fact, the one illustrated was only very slightly deeper than the tiny dyed shells used for the edging.

Ⓓ

Be warned, and do not set a photograph cut from a newspaper or magazine which has print on the back, for this will certainly show through on the front of the photograph when embedded in the plastic — as you can see from our photograph. This is rather damaging to the romantic illusions!

Start the casting by waxing and setting a very thin layer of plastic in the usual way, and when set, arrange an edging layer — such as the multi-coloured shells in the photograph. These should be placed point down and set in two stages, as they are light and liable to float if the full amount of plastic needed to cover them is poured on straight away.

When the shells are covered and set, cut out your photograph so that it is just a little larger (about $\frac{1}{8}$ in.) all round than the open oval space in the centre of the casting. Put it in place, and cover with a very thin layer of plastic, leaving it to set as usual. When the casting has been released (see photograph D), polish the back as directed, before setting a jump ring with adhesive at the top for hanging.

BUTTERFLY PENDANT

The large, dramatic butterfly pendant shown in photograph E looks most attractive hanging on a long chain and worn with a simple sweater or shirt. Don't be afraid that you will have to catch a butterfly for yourself and then have the gruesome task of killing it before you are ready to begin work! It is often possible to buy single specimen butterflies for craft work and the one used here was one of several mounted specimens picked up for a few pennies in a junk shop.

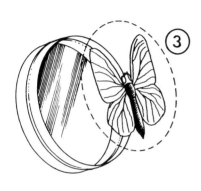

When deciding on a butterfly to set, don't pick one with very pale colours — these tend to go almost completely transparent in the plastic as we found with a beautifully delicate beige butterfly we set at the same time as our pendant was made! This can, of course, look attractive for some purposes, as long as you realise in advance that this is what will happen.

The butterfly we decided to use for the pendant was much too large to fit into any of our commercially made moulds (although larger moulds than those we show are, in fact, available), so we looked round for something suitable to use (see diagram 3). A circular adhesive tape tin was just the right diameter and depth, so we waxed and poured in the first layer of plastic in the usual way.

When setting butterflies, or indeed any insects, they must

be handled with great care as they are very fragile. Use a skewer or matchstick to manoeuvre them very gently into position, and pour the plastic over them a dribble at a time. Leave to set in the usual way.

When the time came to release this particular setting, we realised that there was a moulding in the tin shape which would prevent it turning out. However, as the tin was expendable we were able to saw through it at opposite points on the side and bend the edges back so that the casting could be released (see diagram 4).

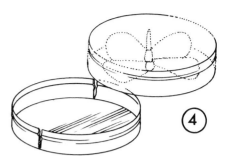

When the casting has been released, finish the back in the usual way. This particular one was left clear, but it would have looked attractive with a layer of crumpled foil stuck on the back. A jump ring was glued to the top to allow the pendant to be hung on a chain. As the pendant was rather heavy, we could have drilled a little way into the top and inserted a small screw ring stuck in with a spot of adhesive. You might think the small extra amount of work worth while for the sake of a stronger mounting.

SEA HORSE EAR-RINGS
The last of the natural objects suggested here for setting is a matched tiny pair of sea horses, each no more than $\frac{3}{4}$ in. long. They were carefully chosen to go together, with tails curled in a similar way, and were measured to fit the 1 in. diameter circular mould shown in the block mould sketched on p.37.

The sea horses were embedded in plastic according to the previous instructions, facing each other, so that when mounted into ear-rings, they could be made to face inwards.

When the castings have set, you can decide whether to put on a coloured backing against which the sea horses will show up or whether to leave the castings clear as we did.

Release the completed casting, polish the back and glue on silver jump rings so that they can be hung on ear-ring mounts as shown in photograph F.

COPPER CHIPPINGS RING AND CHOKER ORNAMENT
We now come to a range of settings from man-made objects, and here again, all kinds of things lend themselves to setting. The ring and choker shown in the colour photograph were simply made from copper chippings, embedded in several layers in two circular mounts, one larger than the other. These copper chippings can usually be bought from craft shops which sell materials for enamelling and plastic settings and cost a few pence for a small bag.

The mould used for the choker was a plastic one with a moulded-in 'lug', so that when the casting is released there is a hole at the top where a mount can be inserted. The mould for the ring was the same one used for the sea horse ear-rings.

Make the castings in three layers, the first a shallow clear one, and the next two with chippings sprinkled in them. This will ensure even distribution of the chippings. If you sprinkled them all in at once, into the full depth of the plastic, they would sink into a mass at the bottom, thus losing the attractive three-dimensional effect.

(G)

When set, released and polished, the casting for the ring can simply be mounted on a copper ring mount as shown in photograph G as if it were a stone (see Chapter 1). To make the choker will, however, require a little more work .

Release and finish the casting in the usual way, but drill into the hole left by the 'lug' so that it is pierced completely through (this can sometimes be done with your skewer, to save drilling).

Next choose a piece of velvet ribbon as a choker, the length to go round your neck, plus 2 inches. We chose a dark brown velvet on which the copper ornament looked most attractive. You will also need a couple of inches of Velcro fastening, or three press studs, and some sewing cotton to match the velvet ribbon.

Turn under and stitch the ribbon 1 in. at each end and sew on the Velcro or press studs. Measure round to the centre front and stitch the casting on, through the hole at the top. Finished choker is shown in colour on page 31.

CUFF LINKS AND RING

If you have an old watch which is beyond repair, you have the basis for a very attractive pair of cuff links and a ring. These are simply made by using the cogs, hands, springs, etc. for the cuff links and using the face and rest of the inside of the watch for a ring. Here's how to work.

First remove the watch from its case. (You will certainly find some use for this in another section of your jewelry making, as you will see later that we did!) Carefully take out the cogs, springs and hands. In the watch we used these were a mixture of gilt and silver.

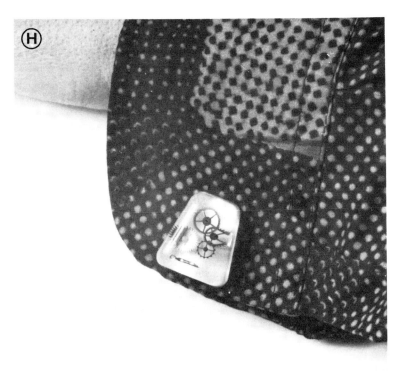

To make the cuff links

As you will see from photograph H, we chose the parallel-ogram-shaped moulds for the cuff links. Before starting to make them, sort the cogs and hands into two groups, trying to work out a balance in the metals and types of springs and cogs between the two links. When this has been done, wax the moulds and put in the first very shallow layer of plastic as usual. Next arrange some of the cogs in each mould, pushing them with a matchstick or skewer into an attractive pattern in relation to each other. Pour over a very little plastic just to cover. When set, repeat, using up the rest of the cogs and again cover with a little plastic. It is necessary to have an opaque backing on this type of cuff link as the metal mount, when stuck on the back, would confuse with the cogs in the casting. We decided to have a white backing layer of plastic as we felt this would show up the cogs to best advantage, but of course, any colour you like may be used.

When the final layer has set, release and polish the castings, and finally mount on flat pad cuff link mounts. We could have chosen either gilt or silver as both metals were in the casting so decide which looks better in relation to your finished castings.

To make the ring

You will see that the interior of the watch now left consists of the face and, backing this, an attractive arrangement of metallic shapes. These may need a little polishing with a proprietary metal polish before setting.

Choose a suitable mould for the ring – we were lucky and found that the watch just fitted into one of the round moulds in our ceramic mould set. Pour in a quantity of plastic and

allow to set. Then put in the watch with the face upwards. Pour in enough plastic to completely cover, then lift up the watch on edge with a skewer and then release it to make sure that no air bubbles are trapped underneath. This in fact happened to our first attempt, and although the resulting casting looked attractive, it is really better to have the watch completely covered with plastic. Leave to set.

You can leave the casting as it is, the flat watch face side being stuck to a ring mount when the casting is released, or you can finish with a coloured layer of plastic if you prefer it. In either case, sand and finish in the usual way before gluing to a ring mount (see photograph I).

SEQUIN PENDANT

Anything shiny set in plastic acquires an added lustre, and some pretty evening jewelry may be made from shaped and coloured sequins.

The pendant (see photograph A) consists simply of five deep pink and one gilt flower-shaped sequins arranged in a hexagonal shallow plastic mould. This is one of the type which, when the casting is released, leaves a mounting hole in the casting, so the sequins were arranged in relation to this.

Before starting work, arrange your sequins in the mould to form the most attractive arrangement, and make sure you place them so that, when the casting is released, the right side of the sequins will show from the domed or right side.

Make the casting and set the sequins in the usual way, and when released, pierce completely through the mounting hole with your skewer or a drill and insert a jump ring for hanging.

HOLIDAY SOUVENIRS

An amusing hobby, which can be carried out over a period of time, is to set various small holiday souvenirs in plastic, either to keep as a collection, or to wear as jewelry. All kinds of things are suitable, coins, stamps, pebbles, flowers, tickets, tiny models — to name only a few (see photograph J).

You could build up enough castings to make a bracelet with the castings hung on a chain, on the same principle as a chain bracelet. Or, using larger objects and castings, hang them from a rouleau belt or mount on a wide leather belt.

The two castings in the photograph on this page, one a stamp and the other a coin are intended as part of a set to mount on a wide belt. Various shapes will be used and in each case the moulds will be the plastic type which leaves the casting with a mounting hole, so that the casting can eventually be stitched to the belt.

Objects should be set in the usual way, extra care being taken with the finishing of the back if you are making castings to hang on a chain bracelet where both sides will show.

5. 'Gipsy' Jewelry From Natural Materials

(See colour photograph on p.51)

It's possible to make a great variety of jewelry, with a gipsy charm all of its own, from natural materials such as stones, cones, bamboo, berries, nuts and even bones (see diagram 1)! However to be attractive to wear, the designs must be well worked out and the mounting and finish good. We have deliberately refrained from showing the traditional little 'bouquets' of beech nut shells, painted and mounted on a pin, which most children make at school at one time or another!

Wear the jewelry from this chapter with informal clothes, trousers and sweaters, cheesecloth smocks, a tweed suit or fur jacket — they will look quite in keeping.

Special requirements are given with directions for making each piece, but in general you will need a supply of mounts, adhesive, Das clay (see chapter 6), paints and a fine paint brush, varnish and a skewer. For working with some of the nuts, a hand drill with a very fine drill will be needed, and also some fine wire.

Above all, you will need a quick eye, to discover the possibilities in the objects you see round you — in the house and garden or on a country walk. A gipsy eye, in fact, to transform natural objects into art!

PEACH STONE BRACELET

The idea for this bracelet (see photograph A) was suggested by a Victorian bracelet seen in an antique shop. The stones had been pierced in order to apply the filigree mounts and they had been dyed dark red before being varnished, otherwise the effect was very much the same. We are fortunate now, however, in having such effective adhesives that much of the laborious piercing and mounting has been done away with.

To make the bracelet, to fit an average size wrist, you will need six medium sized peach stones (add another one if you have a wide wrist); twelve filigree pendant mounts (large size) either gilt or silver; seven large jump rings to match and one spring fastening; varnish and a paint brush.

First scrub the peach stones thoroughly using a stiff bristle brush in order to remove any bits of flesh still adhering to them. Leave them in a warm place overnight so that they are thoroughly dry. Then give two coats of varnish, allowing the first to dry before applying the second, and making sure that the varnish has penetrated all the cracks and convolutions in the stones.

When quite dry, press a filigree mount on to the pointed end of each stone so that the point comes up into the mount as far as possible. Apply adhesive to the inside of the mounts and the stones and stick together. Leave in the salt pot to set.

Next press the mounts in place at the other end of the

stones. These ends are rounded instead of being pointed, but do not press the filigree down to take on this rounded shape. Try to keep the mounts pointed to match the other ends of the stones and merely press the prongs of the mounts so that they will hold the stone. Apply adhesive to the stones and prongs of the mounts and stick in place, allowing to set as before (see diagram 2). Make sure that the rings on the top of the mounts lie in the same plane at each end of the stone, as shown in the diagram, before leaving to set.

When quite firmly set, join the stones together by passing a large jump ring through the mount rings and closing with the pliers (see diagram 3).

At one end use a jump ring, at the other a jump ring and through this a spring fastening to complete the bracelet.

COB NUT BROOCH

The little brooch shown in photograph B is, in fact, an old one, but would be easy to copy for wear on a coat or tweed suit.

You will need a brooch with a spray of leaves in metal — look for one in a chain store or junk shop; a filigree pendant mount to match; a large jump ring; adhesive; some fine wire; and a well-shaped cob nut. (The brooch in the picture was, in fact, pierced to hold the mount, but there is no need to do this.)

Polish the nut with a little wax polish (but not where the mount will be stuck or the adhesion might be affected), or varnish. Press the filigree mount on the flat top part of the nut, bending the prongs well round and making sure that the ring faces open to the front surface of the nut. Stick with adhesive on both nut and mount, and leave in the salt pot to set.

When set, put a jump ring through the mount ring and nip tight with the pliers. Tie on to the bar of the brooch with wire, in such a way that the wire and ring will be hidden by the leaves when the brooch is worn.

PRIMITIVE ARMLET

The splendidly barbaric armlet shown in photograph C would look marvellous with a mediaeval fancy dress — or for theatrical costume jewelry. This is an idea worth remembering for the latter, where large bold effects are needed — at little cost.

All you will need to make the armlet is clay (see p. 61), a quantity of plum stones, if possible in two sizes; and copper and coloured plastic enamel paints, paint brush and adhesive.

First roll out a piece of clay with a rolling pin to make an oblong eleven inches by about two and a half inches. Curve this round to form a bracelet shape, dampen the edges of the clay where they meet and press firmly together, flattening the join as much as possible so that it will not show. With a knife, make small decorative cuts round both edges (see diagram 4).

Before the clay sets, press the plum stones into the armlet to form a pattern. In this case, we used a simple flower shape, then alternated one large and two small stones, as shown.

Take the stones off and you will find that they have left definite indentations in the clay (see diagram 5). Allow the armlet to set, then paint it inside and out with two coats of copper paint, allowing the first to dry thoroughly before applying the second.

49

Paint the plum stones using plastic enamel paints. We used yellow for the centre stone of the 'flower' and white for the 'petals'. The large surrounding stones were blue and the smaller ones green.

When the stones have dried, stick them on the armlet using adhesive. Wear the armlet — which has to be rather wide in order to go over the hand — pushed well up your arm.

AMMONITE RING AND BRACELET

You may be lucky enough to find attractive fossils if you live in the right part of the country. If not, they are cheap to buy in specialist shops, and make an attractive addition to your natural jewelry.

The photograph D on page 50 shows a very simple way of displaying a matching pair of ammonites. One is stuck with adhesive on a plain ring mount and the other on the display pad of a wide steel bracelet. In each case, the ammonite was varnished to give it lustre, but you may prefer to leave your fossils plain.

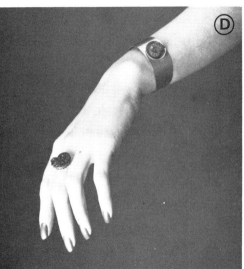

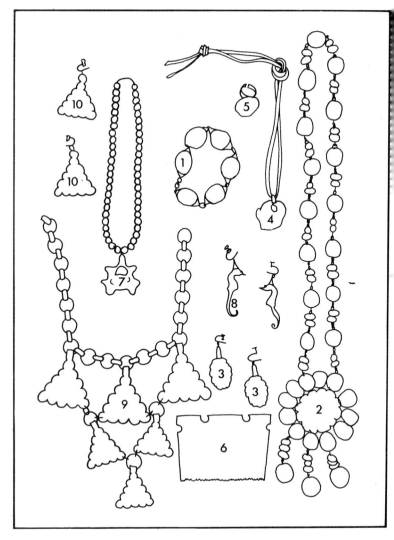

Key to colour picture
1. Peach stone bracelet
2. Acorn and bean necklace
3. Fir cone ear rings
4. Stone pendant
5. Stone ring
6. Wooden comb with berries
7. Golden bone pendant
8. Natural sea horse ear rings
9. Bamboo collar
10. Bamboo ear rings

ACORN AND BEAN NECKLACE

A really 'important' necklace can be made from dried acorns and beans (see photograph E). However, you will, to make it, have to be prepared to drill holes through the beans and acorns using a fine drill (or persuade some handyman you know to do it for you!). It is rather more complicated than the things described so far in this chapter, but the finished effect is worth the trouble.

Materials you will need are: thirty acorns; sixty-five small red beans (or any other colour you like – visit your local delicatessen and see what they have to offer); a round wooden bead about one inch in diameter and with a depth of about a quarter of an inch; a roll of medium thickness wire.

It is best to do all the drilling (see diagram 6) of the acorns and beans at the beginning, rather than piercing holes in them as you need to use them. Using a very fine drill, make holes in all the acorns from top to bottom and in the beans from side to side, as shown. It will help if you can get someone to hold them for you while you drill. You will also need to drill six times right through the thickness of the bead from side to side, going through the centre point each time, but on a slightly different plane as a wire has to be threaded through the bead from side to side so that eventually twelve wire ends project at equal intervals round the bead.

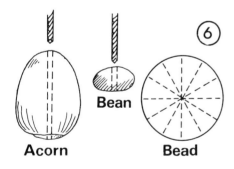

Acorn   **Bean**   **Bead**

⑥

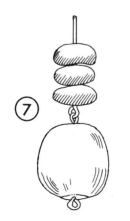

⑦

⑧

52

When the drilling has been completed, you are ready to start making up the necklace. In effect, this consists of three parts: the long 'chain' to go round the neck, which is made up of two beans and one acorn threaded alternately; the circular hanging piece made from the wooden bead surrounded by two circles of beans and one of acorns; and three hanging pieces consisting of three beans and one acorn.

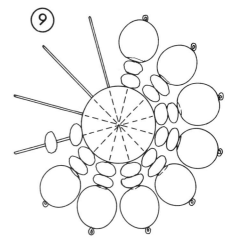

First make the three hanging pieces, as follows. Cut a piece of wire about two inches long and bend one end over to form a loop about an eighth of an inch long. Thread three beans on the wire and leave the straight end as it is for the moment. Repeat with two more pieces of wire. Cut a piece of wire about one and three-quarter inches long and make a loop of an eighth of an inch at one end with the pliers. Thread an acorn on this and trim the wire to a quarter of an inch at the other end. Thread through the loop at the end of the three-bean threading, and bend over to form a loop. (This gives a hanging piece of three beans with an acorn hanging below as shown in diagram 7). Repeat with two more acorns, attaching them as before to the threaded beans. Set these three pieces aside until later.

Now make the neck 'chain' working in the same way as above, but threading two beans on a length of wire, then one acorn, then two beans, and so on. The wires of each pair of beans or each acorn are linked together, to form a continuous chain as shown in diagram 8. Sixteen pairs of beans should be linked to fifteen acorns, beginning and ending with a pair of beans, the ends of the wires left unlooped, so that the neck chain can be fastened to the circular hanging piece when you come to assemble the necklace.

Finally, make the circular hanging piece as follows. Cut six pieces of wire five inches long. Loop one end of each piece of wire over one eighth of an inch and thread on it an acorn and two beans.

Take one of the wires and push it right through the centre wooden bead, and at the end where it comes out, thread two beans and an acorn. Trim the wire end to a quarter of an inch and loop over with the pliers so that the beans and acorns are held firmly against the bead (see diagram 9). Repeat with the other five wires to form the circular motif as shown.

Now assemble the necklace. Cut the wires on the two ends of the neck chain to a quarter of an inch and hook on to two of the acorn wires in the centre motif, leaving one acorn between. Loop round and close with pliers. Hang the three hanging pieces from the three lower acorns and pinch the wires closed.

FIR CONE EAR-RINGS AND BROOCH

It's always a temptation to collect fir cones when out on a country walk, but somehow one never knows quite what to do with them at home and they usually end up in the dust-bin or on the fire. However, carefully chosen specimens make attractive jewelry and we show here two different types of cone which we have used as ear-rings and a brooch (not a matching set).

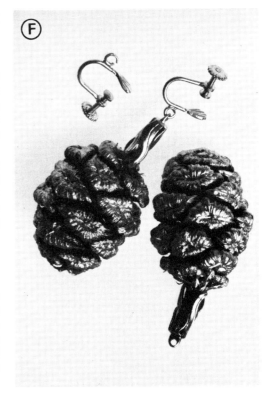

To make the ear-rings

Choose a well-matching pair of cones, each with a piece of branch attached at the top, about half an inch long (trim longer bits of 'stem' to this length). The cones we used were themselves about one and a half inches deep. You will also need a pair of gilt bell caps with long prongs, a pair of screw-on ear ring mounts with hanging rings, adhesive and gold paint and a brush.

Make sure the cones are clean, then paint all over with gold paint, except for the indentations on the cones.

When dry, press a bell cap over each cone's stem, remove and coat stem and inside of cap with adhesive. Stick together and leave to set. When firm, hang a cone on each ear-ring mount, and nip the ring closed (see photograph F).

To make the brooch

For this, use three small cones as shown in photograph G. The ones we found were about an inch long. Pick them with a little piece of branch attached so that this can be stuck to a brooch mount.

Key to colour picture
1. Fabric belt fob
2. Cord and bead bracelet
3. Blue and red necklace
4. Leather and bead head band
5. Primitive bead choker
6. Simple clay bead bracelet
7. 'Indian' mirror pendant
8. 'Indian' mirror ear rings
9. Tiny bead pendant
10. Copper bead ring

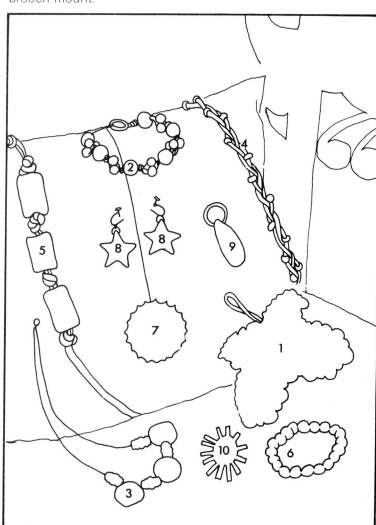

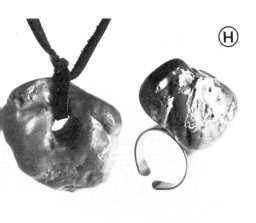

Take an oblong brooch mount and arrange the cones on it until you have decided how they look best, trimming the bit of branch as necessary. Then paint the branches with copper paint, and paint the mount to match if you have not been able to obtain a copper one. Just touch the edges of the cones with copper paint to bring out the shape, and leave to dry.

When dry, stick the cones in place on the mount. We found it necessary to tie them in place with thread to hold the design we had planned, until the adhesive had set. The cotton was then cut and removed.

STONE PENDANT AND RING

Stones from the beach, not tumble polished like the ones in the first chapter, but mounted just as they are can be used to make effective jewelry — but you must search for exactly the right specimens.

The ones in photograph H were found on an East coast beach and are a good match in colours (grey and soft orange tones) and texture. The stone for the pendant had a natural hole in it, and the ring stone a decorative white deposit on the upper face.

To make the jewelry, wash and dry the stones thoroughly, then apply two coats of clear varnish, allowing the first to dry before painting on the second.

Cut a length of leather thonging about two feet six inches long, put it through the hole in the stone, keeping the ends even, and tie a knot to hold the stone in place. Knot the loose ends, and the pendant is complete. Mount the other stone on a ring mount, with adhesive, and leave to set. As the stone will be heavy, allow the adhesive to 'cure' for the maximum time before wearing the ring.

WOODEN COMB

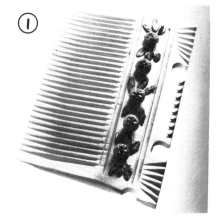

A really gipsy decoration for a carved wooden comb such as the one in photograph I would be real leaves and berries — which is what we used. Do not expect this decoration to last for any length of time — although you will find that the leaves will stick and stay unwrinkled for longer than the berries. However, you can always remove them when no longer fresh and replace with beads or other decoration.

Choose tiny evergreen leaves and small red berries and first coat them all over in clear varnish. Give the comb a coat of varnish too. When all are dry, coat the plain band along the top of the comb with varnish and arrange the leaves as shown in paired groups of three. Between each three leaves stick a berry. Press all gently down with a skewer, then drop more clear varnish on top from your brush to help stick the leaves and berries down more firmly. Leave until the varnish is quite dry.

GOLDEN BONE PENDANT

Would you guess, if you hadn't been told, that the expensive-looking chunk of 'gold' hanging on the pearl necklace (photograph J) started life as a vertebra in a lamb stew! Perhaps you'd better not tell your friends until *after* the party.

To copy, buy a string of cheap pearls from a store or second-hand shop (the one in the picture cost only 5 pence from a tray of old bead necklaces). Try to choose ones which have a creamy or golden look rather than a silvery pearl.

Pick a bone of good shape which is complete and has no bits knocked off it, and wash thoroughly in hot water, scrubbing with a stiff bristle brush to make sure it is completely clean. Leave overnight in a warm place to dry.

Paint the bone with two coats of gold paint back and front and allow to dry, then stick a gold bell cap on the pointed top part of the bone with adhesive.

When the adhesive has set, fix the bone pendant with a jump ring in the centre of the pearl necklace.

NATURAL SEA HORSE EAR-RINGS

Another way of using sea horses for ear-rings (see photograph K) is shown here. The sea horses are considerably larger than the ones set in plastic; in fact they measure two inches in length.

You will need two well-matched sea horses, two tiny gilt filigree bell caps, two gilt ear-ring mounts with hanging rings, two large gilt jump rings and adhesive.

Press a cap on the projecting lump on the head of each sea horse to take the shape, then stick on with adhesive. Leave to set in the salt pot.

When firm, hang on a jump ring through the ring on each ear ring mount and nip closed with the pliers. Make sure that the sea horses face towards each other when the ear-rings are worn.

BAMBOO COLLAR AND EAR-RINGS

A very exotic 'collar' necklace can be made simply from some lengths of bamboo, an old gilt chain belt and a few jump rings. Make a pair of matching ear-rings to go with them for a rather dramatic set (see photograph L).

The materials you will need are as follows: some lengths of bamboo, some about half an inch in diameter, the rest about a quarter of an inch in diameter, or a fraction more; a chain belt similar to the one in the picture; a quantity of large size gilt jump rings; two gilt ear ring mounts with hanging rings; adhesive — any good wood glue would be suitable. You will also need a small saw to cut up the bamboo.

Working on an old piece of board, cut off pieces of bamboo a quarter of an inch long as follows: forty-eight of the larger diameter bamboo and eighty of the smaller diameter bamboo.

Using the larger bamboo pieces, make up three triangular shapes as shown, starting with a row of five pieces at the bottom and working up to one piece at the top. Above the top piece, place another piece of bamboo going the other way

Key to colour picture
1. *Mixed colours on buckle and bracelet*
2. *Pendant on solid band*
3. *Triangular pendant*
4. *Square green and yellow ring*
5. *Grape pendant*
6. *Initial brooch*
7. *Venetian glass bead ring*
8. *Brooch with Venetian glass beads*
9. *Cloisonné belt fob*
10. *Ring to match fob*

58

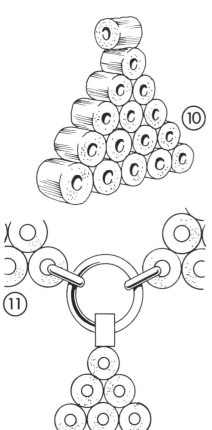

⑩

⑪

(see diagram 10). Stick the pieces together with adhesive and leave to set. Make up three similar shapes from the smaller size bamboo and stick together.

For the ear-rings, make two shapes from small bamboo, but stick the hanging piece for these facing the same way as the rest of the pieces.

When all the shapes have set, rub over back and front with fine sandpaper to smooth off any sharp edges and varnish over all with clear varnish. You could, of course, paint the bamboo shapes if you preferred.

To make up the necklace

Detach a length of chain long enough to go comfortably round the base of your throat and fix on the fastening from the belt at each end (or do this when the necklace is completed). Count out the seven central large links and open up the outer ones at each end and the one in the middle. Thread these links through the topmost links of the three large triangular shapes, and close up with the pliers.

Put large size jump rings through the corner rings of the bamboo shapes as shown, and through these thread large rings taken from the remainder of the belt. Before closing up the large rings, thread on two of the smaller bamboo shapes. Hang the third shape centrally between these two from the lower, inner rings, in the same way. The necklace is now complete. Diagram 11 shows part of the necklace made up.

To make up ear-rings

Pass a large jump ring through the top hanging loop of the remaining bamboo shapes and hang on ear-ring mounts in the usual way.

6. Beautiful Bead Jewelry

(See colour photograph on p.55)

There's a great deal more to bead jewelry than simply threading a few pearls on a string and adding a fastening at the end! This chapter contains some ideas both for using bought beads of various sizes and for making your own beads. For the latter, we used a special type of clay, sold under various proprietary names (we used Das), which is quick-setting and need not be fired. It is a most useful craft material, and particularly handy for jewelry making. It's easy to work with and not nearly so messy as ordinary clay.

It's very difficult to know what one should choose at the handicraft shop when going to buy beads. We have limited ourselves here to comparatively few sizes and types of bead so that you can try out some ideas and see if you enjoy beadwork before spending a great deal of money on materials. All you will need, besides the clay mentioned above is a packet of tiny seed-like beads in mixed colours, a packet of mixed ceramic beads ($\frac{1}{4}$ in. size) wooden beads, different colours in $\frac{1}{4}$ in. and $\frac{3}{8}$ in. sizes, long copper beads and copper chippings, and some hand-made glass beads for a necklace (not necessarily the same as the ones we used — in fact you would be unlikely to find exactly the same type of bead locally).

You will also require leather thonging, some black and some white silk cord and your plastic enamel paints ready to hand. Jewelry mounts, a pencil, some broken glass and a skewer — and you are ready to begin!

FABRIC BELT FOB

Perhaps the simplest article to start with is the butterfly-shaped fabric belt fob shown in photograph A and in our colour picture. This is based on a hand-embroidered needle holder, bought for a few pence in a large store. Any similar fairly ornate and decorative fabric holder with a well-defined shape would be suitable.

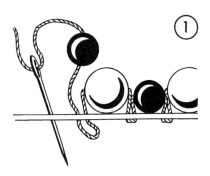

We picked out two of the colours — purple and green — and matched them up in two sizes of wooden bead, and sewed them on to form a decorative edging. To copy, thread your needle with thread colour-matched to the article you are working on, take it up (working it doubled) through the top centre point of the needle case and thread a bead on to it. Poke the needle down to the underside of the case, so that the bead is held firmly in place on top (see diagram 1).

Bring the needle up again to the right side at almost the same point where you put it in. Thread another bead of the second colour and push the needle down again. Continue to work in alternate colours round the article you are decorating, making sure that the beads fall regularly round the outline.

When you have finished, fasten off the thread securely. Our fob already had a cord loop for hanging, but if yours has not, sew a short length doubled so that the fob can be slipped over your belt as a decoration.

CORD AND BEAD BRACELET

Using the same beads as for the belt fob, you can make an attractive bracelet to match it (as shown in photograph B). For an average size wrist, you will need six of the larger size beads and fifteen of the smaller ones. Also required will be a half yard length of three-strand silk cord (we used white with our purple and green beads) and a simple fastening. The one in the photograph was a large gilt 'hook and eye' type taken from an old belt.

Leaving a couple of inches spare at one end, tie a knot in the cord and thread on a large bead, pushing it up to the knot. Untwist the long length of cord and on each strand thread one of the smaller beads (see diagram 2). Push them as far as they will go up to the large bead then tie the three separate strands of cord together in a single knot. Thread all three strands

Key to colour picture
1. Copper pasta ring and ear rings
2. Silver shell pasta pendant
3. Silver pasta and shell wristband
4. Spiral pasta brooch
5. Circular brooch
6. Tear-shaped pendant
7. Ring to match tear-shaped pendant
8. Name pendant

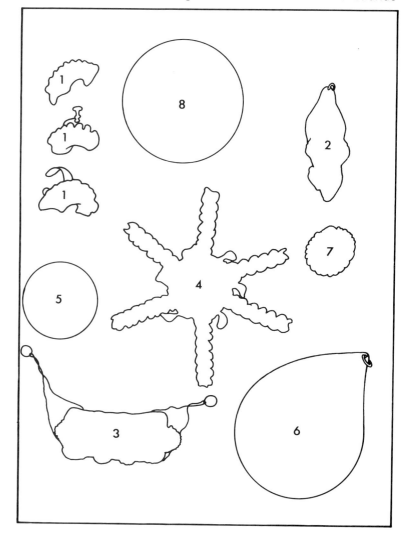

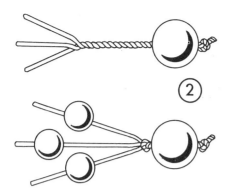

(2)

through the next large bead and tie a knot; then separate them again and thread a small bead on each strand; knot cord as before. Continue working in this way until all the beads are used up, ending with a large bead.

Measure the bracelet on your wrist. If it seems too small, even allowing for the fastening, add another group of three small beads and then another large one before tying the final knot.

Now fasten on the ring at one end and the hook at the other as follows. Take the three strands of cord through the ring and with one strand bind tightly round the other two, taking it round several times. Pull the strand through the last of the loops or turns, pull it tight and trim off. Trim the other two strands of cord off Repeat at the other end of the bracelet.

BLUE AND RED NECKLACE

C

This necklace (see photograph C) is a simple threaded one, its attraction lying in the hand-made Indian beads used as the centrepiece. You will need three large flat beads and four smaller contrasting beads, matched to a quantity of tiny 'seed' beads. You will also require a very fine needle and some strong nylon thread and a necklace fastening.

First tie a knot in the nylon thread, about 2 ins. from one end. (If one knot is not sufficient to prevent the small beads from slipping off, tie two or three more in the same place. Next, using a very fine needle, thread on enough tiny beads to make up a length of six inches. Then thread one of the larger matching beads, next a flat bead, then a matching bead and so on until the seven 'display' beads have been threaded.

Follow with another six inches of tiny 'seed' beads and you are ready to fasten on one end of the clasp. Make sure that the beads are pushed firmly together, then take the thread several times through the fastening ring, knot off and trim the thread. Fix the other half of the fastening at the other end of the necklace.

LEATHER AND BEAD HEAD BAND

D

A similar technique to the wooden bead bracelet may be used to make an unusual head band, but using leather thonging in place of the cord.

For this you will need three lengths of black leather thonging, approximately fifteen inches long, a selection of ceramic beads in different colours, and a piece of black elastic.

Basically, the thonging is plaited and a bead slipped alternately on the outside thong of the plait, as shown in photograph D on this page (completed bead and thong length). The beads should be varied in colour to give a random effect.

You will find it much easier to make the plait if you nail the ends of the three pieces of thonging to a board or piece of wood as we have done (see photograph E). Start to plait the leather, thonging in the usual way, then slide a bead on the right-hand thong before bringing it over to the left. Then slide a bead of a different colour on the left-hand thong before bringing it over to the right (see diagram 3). Continue in this way so that the beads lie alternately on right and left thong (see diagram 4).

When the beaded plait is about twelve inches long, end with

half an inch of plain plaiting to match the beginning. Take the plait off the piece of wood. With a strong needle and black thread, sew across each end of the thonging to hold it together. Then sew the black elastic under the thonging at each end, adjusting it to the size of your own head, so that it will hold the beaded plait across the top of your hair.

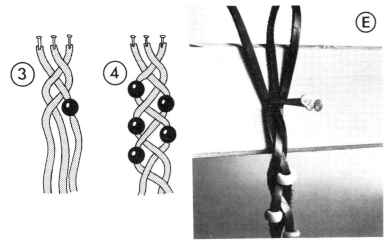

PRIMITIVE BEAD CHOKER

We now come to work with clay, and one of the simplest things to make is a set of large beads which can be painted and used in various ways. Shown in photograph F are three beads being threaded on a thick black silk cord, to form a choker. Experiment with a few beads in this way at first, and if you like the effect you can always extend your efforts and make a belt or long necklace in the same way.

Cut off a chunk of clay and roll it between your hands to form a cylinder about half an inch in diameter and four inches long. Cut this cylinder into three pieces, then take a pencil (a cylindrical one) and push it through the centre of each cylinder of clay, lengthways (see diagram 5). Take cylinders off the pencil and carefully flatten each end. You now have three clay beads, and these can be left in a warm place overnight to set.

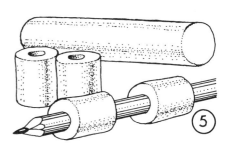

When the beads are completely dry, they can be painted. As they have a chunky, primitive look, it seemed appropriate to copy designs from pottery of the Pueblo Indians of Arizona and New Mexico. However, instead of copying the designs given here you can always find a suitable reference from a book or museum to copy for yourself.

Paint the beads completely in a cream colour (mix yellow and white plastic enamel paints together) and allow this to dry thoroughly. The patterns were copied in black and in a terra cotta (mix red, black, white and yellow paints together until you achieve the right blending) using a very fine paint brush. Study diagram 6 on this page to copy.

When the designs are completely dry, thread on a length of thick black silk cord with a knot between each bead and one at the other end of the two outside beads. Allow enough cord to tie at the back of your neck, knot the cord about one inch from each end and fray out the strands to complete.

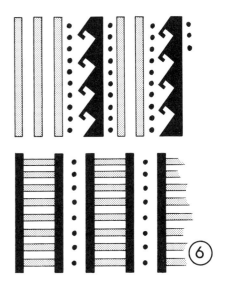

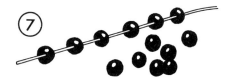

SIMPLE CLAY BEAD BRACELETS

It's easy to make sets of bead bracelets, painted in any colour you fancy — a red one is illustrated in colour.

You will need some lengths of copper wire long enough to go round your wrist and form a hook and a loop at either end for fastening, when the beads are finished.

Cut up a piece of clay into small pieces and roll in the palms of your hands to form round or oval beads. Thread by pushing the copper wire through the centre of each, but do not allow the beads to touch each other (see diagram 7). When each wire is filled, allowing about a half inch at each end for fastening, leave the beads in a warm place to dry. When they are dry, work up and down the wire a little to loosen them, then run off the wire and paint in the chosen colours. If all the beads on one bracelet are to be the same colour, there is no need to unthread them. Simply loop the wire at each end and hang the bracelet up on threads and paint or spray them a uniform colour.

INDIAN MIRROR PENDANT

We now come to a slightly more elaborate use of clay and beads to form an attractive circular pendant with a central bit of mirror glass surrounded by different coloured ceramic beads (see photograph G).

Besides the clay, you will need eighteen red beads, four blue ones and four white ones, a bit of broken mirror glass which will give you a central circle of about five eighths of an inch diameter, silver paint, adhesive and a small silver jump ring. You will also need a circular pastry cutter two inches in diameter.

Roll out a piece of clay with a milk bottle or rolling pin to one eighth of an inch thick and cut out two circles with your pastry cutter. From the centre of one of them cut a small circle about five eighths of an inch diameter, using a thimble or bottle top of a suitable size (see diagram 8). Now place the bit of mirror glass in the centre of the unbroken circle and lay the other circle on top so that the mirror shows through the central hole. Make sure that the serrated edges of both circles match one on top of the other and then press the circles of clay firmly together.

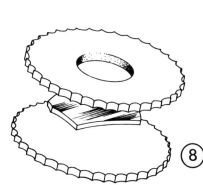

Before the clay has time to set, press a jump ring into the edge between the circles of clay at one point, so that the top edge of the ring protrudes for hanging the pendant on a chain when finished. Another jump ring will have to be fixed through it for this purpose eventually.

Next press a circle of red beads round the edge of the mirror and then a circle of mixed coloured beads round the outside edge — these can be arranged in alternate colours or at random. You will find that the beads will not stick to the clay, but will make a depression which will hold them more firmly when they are later fixed with adhesive. Take the beads off the pendant and leave it overnight to set.

When it is set, paint it with silver paint and allow to dry. Then stick the beads back in place with adhesive and fix the hanging jump ring through the one set into the pendant. When the adhesive has set, the pendant is ready to wear.

INDIAN MIRROR EAR-RINGS

The pretty little star ear-rings shown in photograph H are made from clay, broken mirror glass and little seed beads in green and blue. To copy you will also need two large silver jump rings, silver paint and a pair of silver ear ring mounts with rings for hanging pendants. You will also require a miniature star-shaped pastry cutter (see Chapter 2).

First roll out a piece of clay to about an eighth of an inch thickness and cut out two star shapes with your cutter.

In the centre of each, press a tiny oblong piece of mirror glass so that the clay takes its shape, then remove.

Open two jump rings and press one end of each carefully through the point of the star which comes at the top of the mirror glass (see diagram 9). When you have worked the rings through the stars, close carefully with your pliers. Allow the clay stars to set.

Coat the front of the stars with adhesive and stick the bits of mirror in place. Then stick the tiny beads, making sure that they overlap the central mirrors fractionally to hide the edges. Make a random mixture of blue and green beads, using rather more blue than green.

Allow the adhesive to set, then paint the sides and backs of the stars with silver paint before hanging on the ear ring mounts.

TINY BEAD PENDANT

The multi-coloured pendant shown in photograph I was made from a piece of clay, a mixture of seed beads and a thick ring mount taken from an old chain belt.

First cut off a piece of clay and form it with your hands into a pear shape. Work the mount through the top of the 'pear' and leave the clay to set.

When set, coat the pendant in adhesive and roll it in a heap of mixed coloured beads so that they stick all over it. Fill in any bare patches on the pendant by hand with the beads. Allow to set.

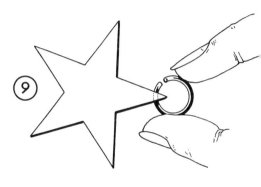

COPPER BEAD RING

Copper chippings and long copper beads were used for the sun-ray ring illustrated in colour on page 55. You will also need a small lump of clay, some copper paint, adhesive, and a copper ring mount.

Cut out an oval of clay about a quarter of an inch thick, one and a quarter inches long and an inch wide (use an oval cutter or mould if you have one roughly the right size). Press with the fingers so that the top surface is slightly domed.

Now push long copper beads all round the outer rim of the clay to give a sun-ray effect. Push smaller copper chippings in the centre. The clay will not hold the copper pieces, so remove them until it has set. When set, paint the whole of the clay shape with copper paint.

Now, with a cocktail stick, drop a little adhesive in the indentations made by the copper beads and chippings and stick these in place. Leave overnight to set.

Finally stick the sun-ray 'stone' on a copper ring mount with adhesive in the usual way.

67

7. Enamel Jewelry

(See colour photograph on p.59)

The craft of enamelling is an old one, and beautiful examples of enamel work may be seen in museums and in the shops. Many people are now attending classes to learn the work for themselves — and of course this is one way of finding out whether it is a craft which appeals to you before going to the expense of buying a kiln to use at home.

Another way is to try your hand at cold enamelling — a new craft which can produce very much the same effects as traditional enamelling. In this way, you can experiment with jewelry making at very little cost and we show you in tis chapter some of the techniques you can use.

What to buy and how to use it

Perhaps the most convenient way to start on cold enamelling is to invest in a complete 'Enamelcraft' or similar kit. These are readily available in craft shops and consist of the following: basic plastic liquid, hardener, twelve pots of colour, including opaque, translucent and metallic colours, measuring spoon and cup, aluminium foil cups for mixing, mixing sticks and paintbrush. All the items may be bought separately if replacement is necessary later on. You will also need a supply of mounts — either new or old jewelry which can be used as a basis for new designs. The makers say that hard surface coatings can be produced on almost anything from glass, metal, china, wood, stone and plastic to such unlikely bases as cardboard, paper and cloth. However, we have concentrated mainly on metal mounts for the purpose of this chapter as these are readily obtainable and most likely to be used.

As with the plastic settings mentioned in chapter 4, people with sensitive skins should be careful to wash their hands immediately if they get any of the plastic or hardener on them, using warm soapy water.

Instructions are enclosed with the plastic, but it may be useful to have them listed in this chapter in case the instruction sheet is mislaid.

Make sure first of all that your working surface is covered with newspaper as the plastic will stick firmly to any surface and it is not desirable to clean it off a polished table with cleaner or varnish remover. Work, if possible, in a warm room which is free from dust; dust settling during the drying process can spoil the fine gloss finish of your work.

The basic mixture of plastic and hardener consists of two parts of plastic to one part of hardener. Measure these with a measuring cup or teaspoon and mix together very thoroughly with a mixing stick or matchstick until the mixture is quite clear.

For your first experiments with the plastic, pour a little of the clear mixture into several aluminium foil cups or other disposable containers and add a different colour to each one. Only a small quantity of colouring agent is needed when using the translucent colours, but more for opaque colours. The metallic colours come in powder form and only a little is needed.

Thoroughly mix the colours into the plastic using separate mixing sticks or matchsticks and they are ready to use. They should be liquid enough to use for three to five hours.

To practice, first work on small flat surfaces, using a brush or stick to apply the enamel (the brush can be cleaned afterwards with the special cleaning fluid or white spirit or nail polish remover and we found the brush generally easier to work with). Make sure before starting work that the surface is clean and free from grease, and spread on only a thin layer of enamel or it may run over the edges. If you wish to apply a thicker layer, allow the plastic to set for an hour or so before using, or make a vertical wall round the base you are working on, using self-adhesive tape. Run in the required amount of plastic and allow to harden, then remove the tape and smooth off the sharp edge with fine sandpaper. Paint over the sanded parts with liquid clear plastic to give a gloss finish.

If you want to work on a slightly curved surface (such as you will find in some brooches or ring mounts), let the plastic set slightly before applying, or you will find that it runs off, leaving the centre of the mount bare.

Make sure that any crystals of plastic which form on the tops of the containers are wiped off and do not fall into the liquid, and made sure that the tops of the bottles are not mixed or you will never be able to unscrew them!

The plastic enamels will take about a week to become completely hard, but you should be able to handle the jewelry after about a day. It is not advisable to try and speed up the setting process by using very high temperatures at first, but once the plastic has initially set, it will harden more speedily if you place the article on or near a radiator or hot water cistern.

We found, in fact, that some colours hardened more readily than others — for instance, green, blue and white were better 'setters' than yellow or red which often took more than a full week to harden. If, after experiment, you find the same problem, add a little more hardener to the basic mixture and make sure that you use the minimum of colouring pigment to achieve the colour you require.

Some suggestions

Many beautiful effects may be achieved by using a mixture of colours, running them on to a mount at the same time and then passing a mixing stick or needle several times through all the colours. You will find that the colours will gradually run into one another before setting.

Don't try to use too many colours at a time — three should be quite enough and, in fact, by the blending of three colours you will end up with several more than that.

You can, if you wish, simply drop the colours on to the surface and allow them to blend naturally without using the

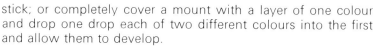

stick; or completely cover a mount with a layer of one colour and drop one drop each of two different colours into the first and allow them to develop.

When the first layer of colour on a piece of jewelry has hardened, you can paint on any other enamel colours you wish to form a pattern. Or drop small quantities of the coloured plastic on a piece of plastic sheeting and allow them to hardening completely. Use the little 'jewels' so formed to press in the surface of unset enamel to give a raised and multi-coloured effect.

In fact, many objects may be embedded in the surface of your jewelry to produce a variety of effects. Little beads, sequins, bits of glass, etc. should be placed on the plastic surface and pressed gently in before setting. The set surface may be painted over with clear plastic afterwards if you wish.

Another technique which is fascinating to try is 'cloisonne' work, and it was in this way that we made the belt fob which is shown in colour on the cover. It is rather more complicated than the techniques described above, but the effects are very attractive.

Basically, thin copper wire is bent to form a pattern or picture and this is then stuck to a suitable mount, using clear plastic. When the wire has stuck, different colours are poured or painted in the sections of the pattern.

These are only a few of the ideas for using plastic enamel and you will find, as you experiment with the glorious range of colours, that you will evolve others which are equally interesting. Here are just a few designs to start you off.

BUCKLE AND BRACELET

As a first experiment, start with some simple mixing of colours to get the feeling of enamel work. You will need a metal buckle and a wide bracelet with a round or square display pad to copy the designs shown here (see photograph A). You will also require a paint brush, a mixing stick, a needle and a small quantity each of red, yellow and blue plastic enamel.

Make sure the buckle and display pad of the bracelet are clean and free from grease, then start work on the buckle, as follows.

With the brush, paint a thin layer of red paint all over the buckle, then with the mixing stick drop small quantities of blue enamel into the red, at random. Using the needle, swirl the blue paint about slightly — this need not be done very vigorously as the colour will soon run by itself. Next, with the other end of the mixing stick, drop yellow enamel in a similar way and run the needle through the colours (see diagram 1).

You will find that the colours develop most attractively, the mixing of the blue and yellow producing plenty of green in the pattern, and the blue mixing with the red to give purplish undertones. So, a typical enamel surface is produced with an interesting depth and variation in colours. Leave the buckle to harden in a warm (but not hot) place. To avoid dust settling on a large flat surface such as this, an old cup or saucer can be inverted over the buckle. Dust settling over a period as long as a week would certainly spoil the glossy finish. If by any chance this does happen during your enamel work, you can, to a

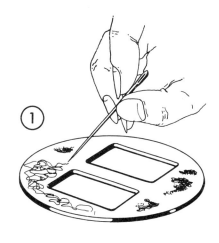

certain extent, retrieve the situation by giving the surface, when quite dry, a coat of clear plastic enamel and leaving to dry under cover as suggested.

Decorate the bracelet pad in a similar way; you can, if preferred, vary the colour emphasis by using the plastic enamel colours in a different order. As the display pad on the bracelet tends to be slightly concave, allow the plastic enamel to harden slightly before using it, or you will find that the colours will tend to run into a pool in the centre. When the colours have been applied, leave the bracelet to set in the salt pot as usual.

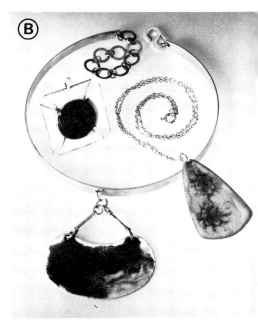

THREE PENDANTS

The three pendants shown in photograph B show the different effects which may be obtained very simply on different types of pendant mount.

Pendant on solid band

First coat the pendant with white plastic enamel to show up the brilliance of the enamel colours to be applied later, and put on one side to harden. When completely set, mix a small quantity of blue, green and yellow enamel and apply a thin layer of blue over part only of the pendant. Next use yellow on the rest of the pendant, but leave a small unequal margin of white showing round the edges. Lastly drop a little of the green enamel to one side of the blue and where the blue and yellow meet.

Now using the needle, mix the colours together a little so that there is some running, but allowing irregular 'blocks' of fairly solid green, blue and yellow to remain. Leave to harden.

Pendant cross

This mount was treated rather austerely as far as colour goes, and the arms of the cross and the hanging loop were given a coat of white plastic enamel, whilst the centre circle was done in metallic copper. Into this was dropped a little gold powder which was lightly mixed with a needle. When the whole pendant has hardened, paint over the centre circle with a very thin layer of metallic copper to give depth to the gold decoration. Allow to harden fully.

Triangular pendant

The clear Chinese yellow of this pendant is very characteristic of true enamelling. First coat the pendant with a fairly thick layer of yellow plastic enamel (if your mount is convex, make sure the enamel is slightly set). Then drop two small drops of translucent violet from a mixing stick, one towards the top right of the pendant and the other towards the bottom left.

With your needle, draw small uneven lines outwards from the centre of each spot of violet. You will find that they will spread to form the 'spider's web' type of pattern seen in the finished pendant. Leave to harden completely before attaching a jump ring for hanging.

SQUARE GREEN AND YELLOW RING

The square ring in the colour photograph is made in a similar way to the triangular pendant, the mount being painted thickly with translucent sea green and two spots of yellow

(C)

(D)

(2)

enamel being dropped in it. However, in this case, the second colour was not spread with the needle but simply left to become slightly cloudy round the edges and to dry out completely.

GRAPE PENDANT

Vines and grapes are a basic decorative motif, going back many hundreds of years — so we could not avoid suggesting at least one grape decoration in this book of jewelry!

All you will need to copy the idea shown in photograph C is a circular copper mount, about two and a half inches in diameter and pierced to take a jump ring for hanging; a few pearl beads from an old necklace; a small metal or plastic gold leaf (these can usually be bought at specialist sewing shops or haberdashery counters and are found with the buttons and sequins); white, translucent green, gold and translucent violet plastic enamel.

First coat the mount with white plastic enamel. Leave it to set very slightly for a few minutes and meanwhile sort out enough pearl beads of mixed sizes to form a 'bunch of grapes' and arrange these on a piece of paper, together with the leaf, so that you will have an idea how they will look when stuck to the mount. Nineteen or twenty beads should be sufficient.

Next, using tweezers, transfer the beads to the painted mount, placing them if possible so that they are lying on their sides so that the pierced holes are not so obvious. Stick the leaf on at the top, and set the pendant aside for a day so that the white enamel holds the beads firmly in place.

Mix a little gold plastic enamel, and with a very fine brush, paint in a stylised 'tendril' pattern round the edge of the pendant. Mix some violet and some green enamel and using the same fine brush (cleaning, of course, between use) apply a little translucent violet enamel on the top of each bead 'grape'. Do not use too much enamel as it will run down between the grapes and spoil the effect. With green enamel, paint over the centre of the leaf, leaving the outer edges gold.

Leave the pendant until the enamels have hardened, then do any re-touching that may be necessary to complete.

INITIAL BROOCH

Fun for a child to make, the green initial brooch in photograph D is a simpler version of the grape pendant. In this case, the mount is coated with translucent green, and the initials formed out of pearl beads with no additional colour (see diagram 2).

VENETIAN GLASS BEAD RING

Packets of little Venetian glass beads can be bought at most handicraft shops and are particularly suitable for making plastic setting or plastic enamel jewelry. They come in a delightful range of colours and patterns, like so many tiny boiled sweets — so you can have a completely variegated set of beads, or match colours with a variety of different pattern uses.

They seemed the ideal decoration for a flat copper mount shaped like a flower with six 'petals'. When the enamelling has been completed and the beads set, the whole motif was set on a copper ring mount (see photograph E).

To copy the idea you will need: a copper mount shaped as

shown in the photograph; six Venetian glass beads in assorted colours (but make sure one or two of them contain some blue); some white and a little blue plastic enamel; a paint brush, tweezers and a needle; adhesive.

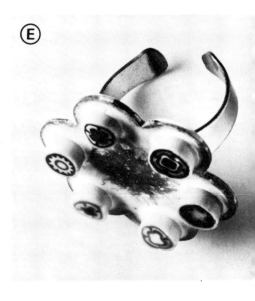

First coat the mount with a layer of white plastic enamel and leave it for a minute or two. Next, place a bead in the centre of each 'petal', pressing it in place. Drop a small spot of blue enamel in the centre of the shape and with the needle run through the colour from the middle outwards, so that a filmy pattern of blue spreads through the centre of the white towards the beads. Leave to harden in the usual way.

When quite set, mount on a ring mount and leave in the salt pot to set.

Brooch with Venetian glass beads

In a similar way, a brooch can be made from the beads, as shown in colour on page 59. Here the background was dark blue enamel and all the beads had patterns in a combination of red, white and blue.

To copy, you will need a shaped brooch mount; several Venetian glass beads; a quantity of dark blue plastic enamel; paint brush and tweezers.

Coat the inside of the mount with a thick layer of blue plastic enamel so that it is almost filled up to the rim and leave to harden completely. When set, paint over with another thin layer of enamel and set the beads in this in an attractive arrangement. Leave to harden.

CLOISONNE BELT FOB

For a first attempt at 'cloisonné' work with plastic enamel, it is necessary to devise a bold pattern which does not contain too much complicated detail. A simple flower or leaf pattern, or a geometric design would be suitable; or copy the belt fob shown here with a bird on it.

To copy the fob (see photograph F) you will need: a large tear-shaped copper mount, pierced at the top for hanging (ours was about three and a half inches long); some copper wire; clear plastic enamel and the following colours — white, green, yellow, red and dark blue. You will also require your jewelry pliers and a paint brush.

First plan the design for the fob, drawing out the bird to size on a piece of paper. Diagram 3 on page 74 gives the exact size of the bird on the fob we used; if you are working on the same size fob, simply trace off the pattern.

Next cut off pieces of copper wire to roughly the correct lengths for making up the individual parts of the bird and bend them to the right shape, using your fingers and the jewelry pliers, and cutting off any excess wire. Each part of the bird should be made separately — for instance, each tail feather, the comb and the head should all be individual shapes. Allow a length of wire for each leg and bend round the ends to form feet.

When all the shapes are satisfactorily formed, with the adjoining points of wire pressed as closely together as possible, set them aside and paint over the entire mount with a coat of transparent plastic enamel.

③

Ⓖ

Then with the tweezers, lift each shaped piece of wire and arrange to form the bird, pressing them down on the transparent enamel. When this has been done, paint over the wires with clear enamel and leave the outline to set firmly for a few days.

Now mix a quantity of dark blue enamel and fill in the background completely, using a fine brush and painting carefully round the wire bird outline. Leave the wire 'legs' uncoated with colour. Allow the blue background to set completely, then paint the body and head in white and the feet and top tail feather in yellow, making sure you leave the outline copper wire showing. It is advisable to allow a setting interval before applying the different colours where they adjoin as it is only too easy to let the brush slip and the colours run into one another. If however, you are impatient and wish to apply all the colours at the same time you can, if the brush does slip over, clean off the colours with acetone or remover supplied with your enamel kit, and start again.

Next apply the red to the comb and central tail feather, and green to the wing and lower tail feather. Leave the pendant to dry and harden completely.

The fob can be mounted on any suitable chain or rouleau belt. The one in the picture was a flat-link chain belt and each oblong in the belt was enamelled one of the colours in the fob in a sequence of red, yellow, blue, white and green. (See photograph G for finished effect).

RING AND EAR-RINGS TO MATCH FOB
The matching ring and ear-rings shown on the model on the cover and on page 73 (see photograph F), were simply made from an old pair of round plastic ear-rings and a circular ring mount. We did not attempt to reproduce the bird design in these small areas, but with a steady hand you could do it, omitting, however, the copper wire outline.

To copy the set, you will need, as well as the mounts, plastic enamel (or use plastic enamel paints instead) in the same colours as the fob, and a paint brush.

Paint the entire ring pad and the two ear rings in blue and allow all to dry. Then paint irregular 'clouds' of the different colours as shown in the photograph, being careful not to go over one colour with another until the first colour is dry. A clear effect is what is required here, rather than the misty effect of one colour running into another. Allow all to dry thoroughly before wearing.

8. Jewelry From Pasta and Pulses

(See colour photograph on p.63)

Pasta and pulses (in which we are including, for the purposes of this chapter, rice, tapioca, split and dried peas, lentils and peppercorns) may sound even more unlikely than orange peel as craft material! However, when looking round the house for an interesting and unusual source of jewelry, our eye lit on the store cupboard. There were jars of pasta contorted into a variety of elegant and curious shapes; would they be too brittle or unmanageable to use? We would see.

Also in the cupboard were packets of rice, sago, lentils (and looking with a fresh eye, we noticed the subtle colour variation in these), barley and other seeds and grains which seemed to have possibilities of colour and texture.

With these as raw material (see photograph A), we contrived a pretty variety of jewelry. Like the orange peel jewelry, this is 'fun' or 'junk' jewelry and will not, of course, be so long-lasting and hard-wearing as the other types we show. However, it is very cheap to make and the mounts can usually be cleaned off and re-used when you get tired of any particular design.

As well as mounts, you will need your metallic paints, clear varnish and white plastic enamel paint, clay, as used for the bead jewelry, adhesive and a selection of pasta and pulses — described with details of making each piece of jewelry.

Generally speaking, the jewelry falls into two categories. The pasta makes bolder pieces and looks best when sprayed or painted with metallic paints. With the pulses and seeds, however, you can achieve a delicate mosaic type of effect and this takes more time to make. You will need a skewer or cocktail stick to manoeuvre the seeds into position and you will find that not only do you need to stick them in position underneath, but you will also have to varnish them when set in order to hold them in place more firmly. The variety of effects you can achieve is wide — for instance, the colour of the base on which the seeds are stuck is important. You will find that rice, for instance, which is translucent looks quite different in each case when stuck on a copper, silver or white painted mount.

It is possible to mark out a rough design on the mount before setting to work on a pulse and seed pattern, but generally you will find that you can lay it out roughly on a table or board first and work freehand on the mount when the adhesive or varnish has been spread on it.

Try some of the designs we suggest before working out ones of your own.

COPPER RING AND EAR-RINGS

These are very simple to make and consist of three 'cock's comb' pastas painted copper and mounted on a ring and two

(B)

screw-on ear-ring mounts (see photograph B).

Choose three pieces of pasta which match nicely, remembering that two of them must face inwards following the curve of the ears for the ear-rings. You will need a copper ring mount and, if you cannot buy copper ear ring mounts (these are more difficult to obtain than gilt or silver) either use silver as it is, or paint the mount with copper paint and allow to dry.

The pieces of pasta themselves should be carefully painted, first on one side and allowed to dry, and then on the other. Paint also inside the hollow end of each pasta. You can, if you wish, fill this hollow with clay, allow it to set, and paint over when dry.

Carefully stick the pastas on the mounts. In the case of the ring, the length of the pasta should go along your finger. The ear-rings should be made so that the pastas follow the curve of the ears and face in towards each other. Allow the adhesive to dry and set very thoroughly before wearing the jewelry.

SILVER SHELL PENDANT

For the pendant shown in photograph C you will need a piece of clay about the size of a walnut and nine shell pasta pieces, two silver jump rings and silver paint.

First mould the clay with your hands into a drop shape, pointing each end, then embed a jump ring at one end, leaving a loop projecting for hanging (see diagram 1) you will need to put another jump ring through this when the pendant is finished and dry.

Next embed the pieces of pasta in three rows round the clay shape, alternating them as shown in the photograph.

Press the pasta pieces well into the clay, pushing it up slightly round the pieces to make them stick firmly. Leave overnight for the clay to set. Examine the pendant to see that the pieces are firm — if they are not, put a dab of adhesive under the ones that seem loose and allow to set. Paint the pendant all over, clay and pasta pieces, with silver paint and hang on a string to dry.

SILVER WRISTBAND

This is a slightly more elaborate use of pasta, involving, besides clay and a neck chain, a few coloured shells (see photograph D on opposite page).

You will need: an oblong piece of clay about two inches by one inch or a little less, eight pieces of ring pasta and two pieces of shell pasta, eight coloured pearly trochus shells (obtainable from most craft shops), silver paint and a short silver necklace chain.

First mould the piece of clay in a slight curve to fit the shape of your upper wrist, then pierce two holes about a quarter of an inch from each end through the depth of the clay from side to side, as shown in diagram 2.

Whilst the clay is still unset, stick the ring pastas on the top, as shown and the shell pastas on each side, pressing them firmly down in to the clay. The clay should hold the pastas in place, but if one or two are not firm after setting, they can be stuck with a little adhesive.

When completely set, paint all over with silver paint and

(C)

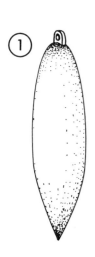

(1)

when this is dry, the coloured shells may be stuck, one in the centre of each ring pasta.

It now remains to make the fastening of the bracelet. Take the necklace chain and cut it in half. Pass one half of the chain through one of the holes in the bracelet pad and the other half through the other hole. If the holes have closed up slightly as the clay has dried and you have difficulty in passing the chains through, enlarge a little with the skewer.

Loop the chain double at each end, and check what length will be needed for your wrist, cutting off any chain which is not required, but making sure that the lengths of chain are even on each side.

Open the ring on the end of the chain and slip the other end of the chain over it as shown. Remove the fastening from the other side of the bracelet and slide this on too. Nip the ring closed with your pliers. On the other side of the bracelet, slide a large jump ring on the chain, fasten the chain with a small jump ring through the two open rings, or use a small piece of wire or fine thread. Slide the fastening into the bracelet pad so that it will not show. The bracelet is now complete. Diagram 3 shows the fastenings.

Other forms of decoration may, of course, be used in the centres of the pasta pieces. Sequins, artificial flowers, beads or gemstones would all be pretty.

SPIRAL PASTA BROOCH

This amusing brooch shows just what can be done with a small chunk of clay and two kinds of pasta (see photograph E) ! You will also need adhesive, a flat pad brooch mount and gold paint and small paint brush. Select six spiral pastas of matching lengths, four shell pastas and break up a couple of spiral pastas into short curly lengths as shown.

Form a small piece of clay into a round 'cake' about one and a quarter inches in diameter and a quarter of an inch deep.

Carefully press the six spiral pastas at intervals round the edge to give a sun-ray effect. Press the four shell pastas in the centre, points together in the middle. Next stick a short spiral between each of the six main spiral pasta pieces and also between the shell pastas on the top of the clay shape. Leave to set overnight.

When the clay as set, test the pastas for firmness of holding, and if any of them seems weak, stick it with a little adhesive. When all is firmly set, paint all over with gold paint (or spray if you prefer it).

Finally stick a brooch mount on the flat side to complete.

CIRCULAR BROOCH

We now come to the jewelry made from pulses and seeds. You will find that these come up in a subtle range of colours from white through cream, beige and brown to light and dark orange, yellow and green. Before starting work, shake a little heap of each kind of seed into a separate saucer; you will find it easier to work in this way rather than having to delve into packets and jars each time. For the brooch shown on page 78, you will need a little of each of the following: long grain rice, barley, tapioca and lentils. Sort out a heap of green coloured lentils from the orange ones.

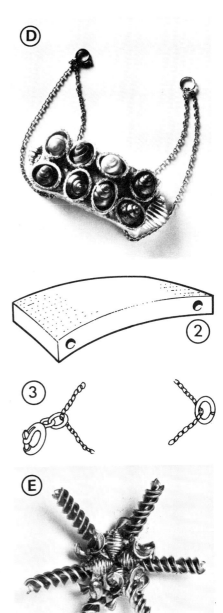

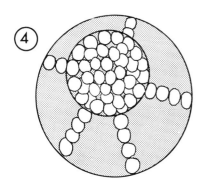

You will also need a circular brooch mount with a central or off-centre raised pad (or use a pendant mount and separate brooch mount, sticking one on the other in the final stages); some clear varnish; a skewer or cocktail stick.

A geometric design is the simplest to begin with, relying for effect on the contrast between colours and textures of the seeds you use.

First coat the whole of the brooch surface with clear varnish to act as an adhesive, then carefully stick orange lentils over the round raised central pad, pushing each into place with your skewer.

Next arrange lines of orange lentils as shown, radiating out from the centre circle and forming five divisions round the brooch (five lines) as shown in diagram 4.

Fill each section as shown: tapioca, barley, tapioca, rice, green lentils. Make sure the seeds are pushed firmly down to stick on the varnish (you will find you have to keep wiping your skewer point with a little varnish remover from time to time or the seeds will stick to it). The seeds may be arranged at random, except that the rice generally will look better if it is arranged with the points of the grains towards to centre, the length of the grains lying parallel.

Allow the seeds to set, then coat with varnish, or spray. This will help them to stay firmly in place. If using a pendant mount, stick this with adhesive on a brooch mount when the varnish on the front is dry.

There is, of course, no need to keep to the arrangement of seeds suggested here – just use any attractive combination from the packets you have in your store cupboard.

TEAR-SHAPED PENDANT AND MATCHING RING
Once you become more expert, you can make quite elaborate designs in seed mosaic. Try your hand at the large pendant and matching ring illustrated here in photograph F, which gives good scope for an intricate and beautiful design.

To make the pendant

You will need a large tear-shaped copper mount (the one used measured three and a quarter inches deep); a large jump ring white plastic enamel paint and a paint brush; the following pulses and seeds – split peas, rice, tapioca, lentils, divided into heaps of orange, yellow, green and brown, barley.

Basically the design is a group of daisy-type flowers of different sizes and formed from different grains, on a white background of tapioca and edged with two rows of orange/green lentils. See in diagram 5 the composition of the different 'flowers' and their arrangement on the pendant in photograph F.

First paint over the pendant with white paint. It is on this surface that the seeds will stick.

Next arrange the first main flower shapes A, using split peas and lentils as shown on key. Then work in Flower B, then all the flowers C and D, and finally the 'rice flowers' shown at E. This gives the main decoration on the pendant.

Stick a line of green/orange lentils in two curves as shown on the key, and finally fill in the background with tapioca.

When the paint has dried, shake the pendant gently to see whether any of the seeds detach themselves. If so, stick back in place with a tiny spot of adhesive or clear varnish. Then clear varnish or spray over the whole pendant. Attach a jump ring through the hole at the top.

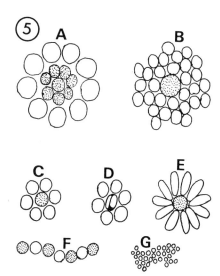

Key to diagram 5

A *Split peas for outside petals, brown lentils for centre*
B *Greenish split pea centre, orange lentil petals (flat side uppermost)*
C *Yellow lentils for outside petals, green lentils for centre*
D *Orange lentils for petals, barley for centre*
E *Long-grain rice for petals, green lentil for centre*
F *Alternate orange/green lentil edging*
G *Spaces filled in with tapioca grains*

MATCHING RING

For the ring you will need green and orange lentils, split peas and tapioca; clay; white paint, clear vanish and a paint brush; a ring mount with flat pad.

For the basis of this ring, you can use the watch case left over after making the plastic settings jewelry (see p.44), simply filling it with clay to form a flat upper surface. Or mould a piece of clay into a round shape about one inch in diameter and a quarter of an inch thick. When dry, paint the upper surface white and arrange a flower A (but using only one central lentil) and a flower C (but use orange lentils for the 'petals') as shown edging the circle with orange lentils. Make a short edging 'sweep' F in green lentils and fill any spaces with tapioca.

When set, varnish as for the pendant. Paint the back of the shape or the watch case gold and stick on a gold ring mount to complete.

NAME PENDANT

Teenagers will like this pendant (see photograph G) with the name of their favourite pop star, boy friend (providing it's short, like Dave, and not long, like Bartholomew!) or their own name spelt on it in peppercorn letters!

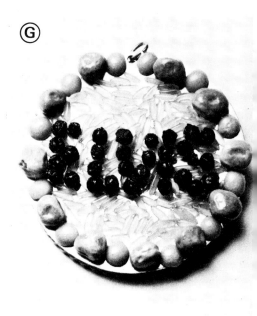

To make it you will need a circular copper pendant mount about two and a quarter inches in diameter; clear varnish and a brush; skewer or cocktail stick; split peas, dried peas, long-grain rice and peppercorns.

First coat the mount with clear varnish, then stick on an edging composed of split and dried peas, used alternately.

Fill the centre with a random arrangement of rice grains so that it is completely filled. You will see that the colour of the copper mounts shows attractively through the translucent grains of the rice. Allow to set and dry.

When dry, coat or spray the entire surface of the pendant with clear varnish and spell out the chosen name in peppercorns. It is advisable to practise with these on a flat surface before putting in position on the brooch (do this first before applying any varnish, too, to make sure that the name fits without being too cramped). When the letters have stuck in position, varnish over as before. Fasten a jump ring through the hole to complete.